THE
Geocaching
HANDBOOK

The Guide for Family Friendly,
High-Tech Treasure Hunting

Second Edition

Layne Cameron
With a foreword by Dave Ulmer

D1115386

FALCONGUIDES

GUILFORD, CONNECTICUT
HELENA, MONTANA

AN IMPRINT OF GLOBE PEQUOT PRESS

To buy books in quantity for corporate use
or incentives, call **(800) 962-0973**
or e-mail **premiums@GlobePequot.com.**

Copyright © 2004, 2011 by Morris Book Publishing, LLC

ALL RIGHTS RESERVED. No part of this book may be reproduced or transmitted in any form by any means, electronic or mechanical, including photocopying and recording, or by any information storage and retrieval system, except as may be expressly permitted in writing from the publisher. Requests for permission should be addressed to Globe Pequot Press, Attn: Rights and Permissions Department, P.O. Box 480, Guilford, CT 06437.

FalconGuides is an imprint of Globe Pequot Press.

Falcon, FalconGuides, and Outfit Your Mind are registered trademarks of Morris Book Publishing, LLC.

Project editor: David Legere
Text design: Sheryl P. Kober
Layout artist: Melissa Evarts

All photos by Layne Cameron unless otherwise noted.

Spot art (maps): Janet Colandrea

A Note about the Maps: The maps within this book highlight actual geocache coordinates. The first set of coordinates on the top line is expressed in the more commonly used World Geodetic System of 1984 (WGS84). The second set of coordinates on the bottom line is expressed in the Universal Transverse Mercator (UTM) system.

Library of Congress Cataloging-in-Publication Data is available on file.

ISBN 978-0-7627-6383-2

Printed in the United States of America

10 9 8 7 6 5 4 3

The author and Globe Pequot Press assume no liability for accidents happening to, or injuries sustained by, readers who engage in the activities described in this book.

To my wife, Sandy, my sons, Alex and Kyle, and to my parents and grandparents, who have helped nurture my storytelling skills and my spirit of adventure.

CONTENTS

FOREWORD

Here we are at the tenth anniversary of the invention of geocaching. Both the number of geocaches and the number of geocachers are in the millions and continuing to grow. It is likely the fastest growing new sport on the planet, but to me there is much more to geocaching than what most people know. What we are witnessing here is another major milestone in the evolution of the human race itself. Other milestones in human evolution like the use of fire, levers, the wheel, writing, and printing may actually pale in comparison to the discovery of the nature of living intelligent systems like geocaching.

Geocaching is just one of millions of other intelligent systems operating here on Planet Earth, but it is distinct in one very important way. Geocaching was the first intelligent system designed to ever understand the true nature of living intelligent systems, like the first fire started by the first scientist who actually understood what fire was. Imagine him lighting that flame and stepping back and saying "I understand that, I know what is actually going on there" in that flame. Knowledge of fire is one thing but "understanding fire" is a whole different ball game. Humans had knowledge of fire for millions of years before they actually understood what it was. They also assembled intelligent systems (a family is an intelligent system) long before they understood what they were building. An intelligent system is simply a system of both knowledge and understanding, and they are as common as dirt. Intelligent systems are most easily identified by words ending in "ing," like reading, writing, walking, talking, sweeping, and washing. Geocaching was the first intelligent system engineered and understood by a human, and designed to be a living intelligent system from the start.

In the world of intelligent systems, "knowledge directs," and it was "new knowledge" that directed development of geocaching. In May of 2000 the U.S. military was directed to remove the jamming signal from its GPS satellite navigation system, and at that moment the world changed. With knowledge of this upcoming event, I stayed awake past midnight watching the screen of my GPS receiver at just the moment when its accuracy increased tenfold. I was awestruck and immediately knew that the human race was just given an additional capability that the general public had never experienced before. For the first time, human beings could locate and relocate positions on our planet with high accuracy. I lay awake that night just brainstorming what could be done with this additional capability. What came to mind was a treasure hunt game and so it became a new intelligent system.

I spent the next day testing and retesting this new location capability. I wanted to be sure that a specific location's coordinates could be recorded and then returned to at a later time with sufficient reliability to make treasure hunting possible. Over the next day I worked out the procedural knowledge needed to play the game, from placing the "stash," what to put in the stash, and what not to put in a stash, to recording and sharing the coordinates and possible locations for the first GPS stash. These were the first efforts to create the knowledge base of what is now called the intelligent system of geocaching.

On the third day of May, I recorded a video of the contents of the first GPS stash, which you can see at www.youtube.com/watch?v=t4VvS_6MaeE, and placed this first GPS stash at the coordinates N45 17.460 W122 24.800 (WGS84). I posted these coordinates on the Usenet newsgroup sci.geo.satellite-nav. Within a couple of days this stash was found and more stashes were being created all across the country. It was an exciting time to see the sport take off so rapidly.

For the next couple of months, I played with the idea in many different ways, trying to flesh out the knowledge base and make it a complete and fully functional intelligent system. I had bad feelings about the name GPS Stash Hunt because of the drug culture connotations of the term "stash." I also wanted the game to be immediately recognized as an activity, like hunting, fishing, flying, or hiking, and this meant that the name needed to end with an "ing" to be a true understanding. At the time most people on the newsgroup were satisfied with the name

GPS Stash Hunt, but I was not and kept demanding that we get a better name. Finally, after two months a member came up with the term geocache, and geocaching. At first, I didn't like it because "cache" was not a word I commonly used, but after studying the dictionary and encyclopedias, I concluded that it was just fine and gave the new name my full support. At that moment, geocaching was born as a fully functional and well-designed living intelligent system.

Geocaching was a catchy name, and being a new activity, it quickly caught fire in many minds. In another month Jeremy Irish caught on the idea of geocaching and registered the name on the Internet as www.geo caching.com. Geocaching is a classic example of how a single human mind can create a huge living intelligent system that now encompasses millions of other minds. We now have a generation of children who have grown up with a GPS in hand and a love for the great outdoors. It is my hope that some of these young geocachers will become the knowledge engineers of the future and be able to look back on geocaching as a shining example of the first intentionally designed and engineered living intelligent system.

Let this handbook be your guide to learning about and enjoying the wonderful world of geocaching. In terms of intelligent systems you will become one of the millions of understanding engines and keep the system alive. Geocaching is an evolving, growing, living,

intelligent system designed to be fun for all who participate. The future human race can look forward to many
more better designed, well-understood, living intelligent
systems like geocaching.

—Dave Ulmer

An electronics and software engineer and self-professed techno-geek,
Dave Ulmer is considered the founding father of geocaching. He lives
in Portland, Oregon.

ACKNOWLEDGMENTS

Thanks to my wife and my boys for supporting me through this entire project and for allowing me to drag them into geocaching and other outdoor adventures time and time again. I'm also grateful to Scott Adams at Globe Pequot Press, who believed in my work and knew I could write this book.

INTRODUCTION

WELCOME TO GEOCACHING! This fascinating, family-friendly, outdoor-oriented pastime is equal parts scavenger hunting, hiking, outdoor adventure, and gift exchange—with a technological twist. This book will provide everything the aspiring geocacher needs to get started.

Seeking hidden treasure, whether it's a friend crouching behind a bush or a pirate's buried gold, has been a universal human quest since the beginning of time. As children, we played hide-and-seek and went on countless scavenger hunts until the last ounce of twilight was milked from humid summer evenings. Now, with GPS units or smartphones in hand, we can rekindle those memories as adults.

Technological advances allow current GPS receivers and smartphones to tell us where we are virtually anyplace in the world with pinpoint accuracy—between 5 and 10 feet. Creative technophiles have incorporated these amazing tools into a treasure-hunting game that has sent millions of people around the world into the wilds to locate geocaches. The first five-gallon bucketful of prizes set out in May 2000 by Dave Ulmer sparked this new pastime. Few of us envisioned how popular it would become.

Fueled by the Internet, geocaching communities have blossomed, continually introducing new people to the activity while simultaneously producing an endless supply of caches for those whose finds number in the hundreds. Dedicated geocachers add new twists to their hobby on a daily basis; new games pop up and are embraced worldwide quicker than you can say, "You're it!" No sooner is a new cache hidden than it is found—many times within hours of being stashed.

This guide will introduce you to all the terms, games, etiquette, and technology you need to get started. So what are you waiting for? Peruse these pages and get started geocaching!

Author Layne Cameron finds yet another geocache and records his name in the logbook.

1

Geocaching:
The Global Sensation

Before we can talk about the birth of geocaching, we must first look at the creation of the satellite navigation systems that made the activity possible.

GPS: A Twentieth-Century Miracle

In the early 1960s, President John F. Kennedy announced his new goal of putting a man on the moon before the end of the decade. The U.S. military, the National Aeronautics and Space Administration (NASA), and the Department of Transportation adopted a "to the moon" mentality and turned their collective attention toward the development of a satellite navigational system. Their objectives for the system included global coverage; continuous usage; all-weather capability; land, maritime, and aeronautical applications; and, of course, high accuracy.

In 1964 the U.S. Navy launched the Navigation Satellite System, better known as Transit, the first space-based satellite system. Since we were in the midst of the Cold War and the space race, the Soviet Union matched these efforts with the creation of its Tsikada system.

Both systems provided the first two-dimensional, high-accuracy positioning service. The major downside to these systems was that it took ten to fifteen minutes for a receiver to process an estimated position. This slow processing was acceptable for maritime navigation because of ships' relatively low speeds, but unacceptable for the high-speed realm of jet airplanes. As the navy began upgrading Transit, the air force developed its own system, and the army also began working on alternative navigational systems.

In 1969 the Office of the Secretary of Defense established the Defense Navigation Satellite System (DNSS) program, whose goal was to consolidate the military's independent efforts into a single, shared system. The Navigation Satellite Executive Steering Committee (NSESC) was created to determine the viability of DNSS. In one of those rare instances of a governmental committee actually doing some good, the NSESC birthed the concept of the Navigation Signal Timing and Ranging Global Positioning System, commonly known as NAVSTAR GPS. (Reviewing the committee's meeting minutes, however, produces no record of discussions related to recreational aspects of the new technology. Apparently, the specter of the Cold War and the race for the moon consumed the members' time and kept them from creating a fun, outdoor treasure-hunting game. For that oversight, we must give the committee an A rather than an A-plus.)

It wasn't until 1978, though, that the first GPS satellite was launched, and it took another six years before President Ronald Reagan announced that a portion of GPS capabilities would be made available to the

Massachusetts Cache
N 42° 00.292 • W 070° 42.884
(WGS84)
UTM: 19T E 357998 N 4651739

civilian community. About that same time, products for civilian consumers began appearing on the market.

Once completed, the GPS system consisted of twenty-four satellites orbiting at about 12,500 miles above the earth in six orbital planes. Each satellite completes one orbit every twelve hours.

Back on the ground, GPS units work by receiving satellite signals, measuring relative arrival times, and computing the location of the user. By receiving signals from at least four satellites, early GPS units could determine three-dimensional geographic coordinates to within 100 meters.

As the United States developed GPS, the Soviets progressed from their Tsikada system roots to create GLONASS (Global Navigation Satellite System), a space-based system quite similar to GPS. Like its capitalistic counterpart, GLONASS was inspired by the military and is still managed by Russia's Ministry of Defense. GLONASS also consists of twenty-four satellites but differs from GPS by using three orbital planes rather than six.

With the Flip of a Switch, Geocaching Is Born

In 1996 President Bill Clinton penned Presidential Decision Directive NSTC-6, America's GPS policy. One of the policy's goals was to incorporate the use of GPS in "peaceful civil, commercial, and scientific applications worldwide."

As a result of this directive, President Clinton ordered the Defense Department to turn off Selective Availability—the jamming signal that prevented recreational users from pinpoint accuracy—on May 1, 2000. The announcement was made via a White House news release: "Today, I am pleased to announce that the United States will stop the intentional degradation of the GPS signals available to the public beginning at midnight tonight. . . . This will mean that civilian users of GPS will be able to pinpoint locations up to ten times more accurately than they do now."

Quite literally with a flip of a switch, GPS users saw higher position accuracy and improved speed or velocity of tracking. Portable GPS units could lock in on a target within 5 to 10 meters. "The decision to discontinue Selective Availability is the latest measure in an ongoing effort to make GPS more responsive to civil and commercial

Thanks to the demise of Selective Availability, GPS units now receive more precise information that can put you within 5 to 10 meters of your target.

users worldwide," wrote President Clinton. "This increase in accuracy will allow new GPS applications to emerge and continue to enhance the lives of people around the world."

As history was being made, self-professed techno-geeks like Dave Ulmer, an electronics and software engineer from Portland, Oregon, followed the announce-ments. Ulmer stayed up late that night just to watch his GPS unit's accuracy improve. "The improvement was dramatic indeed," Ulmer said. "I soon realized that there should be applications for this increased accuracy that were previously impossible."

After brainstorming new ideas for this budding tech-nology, Ulmer came up with the idea of a treasure hunt. The next day he practiced finding locations from various directions, verifying that everything worked. On May 3 he placed a five-gallon bucket near a wooded road about a mile from his home. Inside the bucket were a logbook and some trinkets for trading. He dubbed his game The Great American GPS Stash Hunt.

After tipping off a friend to the location of the stash—to allow his buddy to become the first treasure finder—Ulmer posted a message on the Usenet newsgroup sci .geo.satellite-nav announcing the inaugural stash. (See the original messages on pages 7 and 8.) "Waypoints of secret stashes could be shared on the Internet, and people can navigate to the stashes and get some stuff," Ulmer wrote in his newsgroup posting. He noted only one rule: "Get some stuff, leave some stuff."

THE NOTES THAT STARTED IT ALL

- From: Dave
- Subject: The Great American GPS Stash Hunt!
- Newsgroup: sci.geo.satellite-nav
- Date: 2000/05/03

Now that SA is off we can start a worldwide Stash Game! With non-SA accuracy it should be easy to find a stash from waypoint information. Waypoints of secret stashes could be shared on the Internet, people could navigate to the stashes and get some stuff. The only rule for stashes is: Get some stuff, leave some stuff! The more valuable the stuff the more stashes will be started.

I'm thinking about half burying a five-gallon bucket with a lid at the stash point. Putting in some stuff. Adding a logbook and pencil so visitors can record their find. The log should contain: Date, time, what you got, and what you put in. Scanning the logbook should give you a quick inventory of the stash.

I'll look for a place near a road where few people would normally go . . . put in some cash, an old digital camera, and some antique silverware! I will come up with a cool name for my stash and post coordinates soon!

Make your own stash in a unique location, put in some stuff and a logbook, and post the location on the Internet. Soon we will have thousands of stashes all over the world to go searching for. Have fun!

Dave

- From: Dave
- Subject: GPS Stash Hunt . . . Stash #1 is there!
- Newsgroups: sci.geo.satellite-nav
- Date: 2000/05/03

Well, I did it, created the first stash hunt stash and here are the coordinates:

N 45 17.460
W122 24.800

Lots of goodies for the finders. Look for the black plastic bucket buried most of the way in the ground. Take some stuff, leave some stuff! Record it all in the logbook. Have fun!

Stash contains: DeLorme Topo USA software, videos, books, food, money, and a slingshot!

Not wanting to corner the market, Ulmer encouraged others to follow his lead. "Make your own stash in a unique location, put in some stuff and a logbook, and post the location on the Internet. Soon we will have thousands of stashes all over the world to go searching for. Have fun!"

Less than five days after Ulmer set out the inaugural cache, other caches were placed from California and Illinois to as far away as Australia. And less than a week after the first stash was hidden, Mike Teague, one of the first visitors to Ulmer's cache, created a website as a clearing-house for geocaches. A mailing list was also formed on eGroups (now Yahoo!) by geocachers to share their ideas.

Soon after the caching craze started to grow, the activity's founding fathers decided that a name change was needed. The term geocaching was offered in lieu of stash hunt. Caches began to pop up around the world.

Along with the growth of caches came the growth of Internet sites promoting the new pastime. By September 2000 Geocaching.com, created by Groundspeak and Jeremy Irish, grew into a central forum for geocachers across the globe and quickly usurped Teague's site. Soon other Internet sites like Navicache.com and Buxley's Geocaching Waypoint came online. All these sites act as clearinghouses that publish cache locations, list geocaching clubs, promote forums and events, answer frequently asked questions, and promote geocaching etiquette.

Consumer interest, when coupled with industry interest, has helped fuel the activity's phenomenal growth. Handheld GPS receivers manufactured by Garmin, DeLorme, Magellan, Bushnell, and Lowrance—to name just a few—are pocket size but seemingly have all the bells and whistles of a laptop computer. Before Selective Availability was turned off, receivers could estimate location only to within 100 meters. Now they are able to pinpoint your locale to within 10 feet. Some have two-way radios built in, so you can talk with your fellow geocachers as you seek treasures or play geocaching-related games such as tag, navigating a maze, or whacking lizards that "pop up" from the ground. (Chapter 5 is devoted to these and other games.)

Screens that once resembled bland digital watches now have touchscreen, full-color, and 3-D display capability. Scrolling detailed maps can mark your progress; increased memory allows receivers to store more than 1,000 waypoints, 200 routes, and 5,000 geocaches; some units have integrated cameras that create geotagged images; power cables let you plug your device into a car lighter and preserve battery life; and USB ports and PC serial cable accessories allow quick map downloads.

Other companies are tuning in to geocaching's potential as well. Some firms have handheld GPS units specifically for geocaching. Others made seemingly every map, chart, and aerial photo of the world available to download into your receiver or smartphone. Others are making prizes specifically to be stashed in caches or manufacturing items to help hide caches in, such as fake, hollow rocks.

Not surprisingly, the number of geocaching clubs has grown by leaps and bounds in the United States and worldwide. A list can be found in chapter 8—though it's of course incomplete, because so many new clubs are created seemingly every day. The number of caches will also continue to grow. At the time of publication, there were more than one million active caches placed in more than one hundred countries.

What's exciting about following geocaching since its inception is watching it evolve. It takes on new dimensions almost daily with the introduction of new games, the addition of more Facebook and Twitter geocaching sites, the different twists on traditional caches, the launch of new games, the formation of new clubs, the plethora of innovative technological advances, and the collective shouts of joy as hundreds of newcomers locate their first cache.

If the meteoric growth on so many levels is any indication, geocaching will be enjoyed for many generations to come.

2
Let's Go Geocaching

Now that you know how geocaching was created, it's time to go geocaching. For starters, you will need:

- Access to the Internet.
- A GPS unit or smartphone with GPS capability.

It would also be helpful to have:

- Topographic maps.
- A compass.

You're ready to begin geocaching!

Step 1: Visit the Web

To kick things off, seek out sites such as www.geocaching .com, www.navicache.com, Buxley's Geocaching Waypoint at www.brillig.com/geocaching, or TerraCaching at www.terracaching.com. These are all examples of detailed, all-purpose sites that provide a wealth of information. First and foremost they list numerous caches for you to find. In addition these sites include myriad pages of topics related to geocaching and many links to other sites such as home pages for geocaching clubs that list caches, events, and other useful information specific to your area. (See chapter 8 for additional listings.)

You can register at these sites if you'd like (although you don't need to register to find cache locations). Registration is simple and free and will allow you to post your comments after you find a cache, list caches that you set out yourself, and put you in contact with other geocachers. (You can also sign up for premium membership packages, such as the package available at Geocaching .com.) Typically, when you post your find comments, your e-mail address will be listed next to your username, which is your geocaching nickname.

When it comes to perusing the many geocache listings, these sites allow you to search for geocaches by country, state, zip code, or specific latitude and longitude coordinates. First-time geocachers are usually surprised by the number of caches that can be found within an hour's drive of their home.

Step 2: Select a Cache

Once you've located cache listings for your geographic area, it's time to select a cache. Before you begin, make sure you check the difficulty and terrain rating of each geocache and read the text description of the cache's location. All this information will help you pick a cache that's suited to your skill level.

Start playing by selecting a nearby cache with descriptive clues. This microcache, named "Chief Muncie" after a nearby statue, is great for beginners.

For example, one easy-to-find cache is "Chief Muncie," a microcache listed on Geocaching.com. It's located in Muncie, Indiana, at N 40º 12.290 W 085º 23155. The web page even shows a picture of the statue the cache is hidden near (it's located at a city intersection, so participants' fitness level is not an issue), notes the difficulty and the terrain rating (flat, paved streets and sidewalks), and offers the hint that the container is a tube 2 inches by 12 inches. Clues like these practically ensure a beginner's success.

Step 3: Gather Your Equipment

Once you've selected a geocache that you would like to visit, you'll need a GPS unit or smartphone with GPS

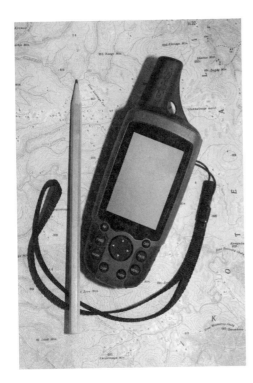

If you're geocaching in an unfamiliar area or in the backcountry, it's a good idea to take a map.

capability. GPS units can range from simple to extravagant, black and white to color, and can range from $70 to $600. For geocaching, you'll probably want to select one that's waterproof or at least has a waterproof pouch in which it can be stored. You'd hate to lose your way because you got caught in a rainstorm or stumbled into a stream and drenched your unit. The capacity to store maps is also a nice feature. And depending on the terrain where you'll be geocaching, find one that has a good antenna. Barriers such as tree canopies, canyon walls, and tall buildings can block signals. (For more information about selecting your GPS unit, see chapter 3.)

Even though you'll have a GPS unit or smartphone, you should back it up with the old reliable map and compass combination. (Regardless of your outdoor activity of choice, it's always a good idea to have a working knowledge of map-reading skills. Think math teacher taking away your calculator before a final exam.) A topographic map will give you a good idea of what type of terrain surrounds the geocache, and it will also help you scout out the best route to your destination. A swamp, a mountain, or a ravine may lie between you and the cache. A level ridgetop trail clearly marked on the map, although not the shortest route, may turn out to be the easiest. The map and compass will also serve as a backup in case your GPS loses its signal due to a dense canopy of trees or conks out because of dead batteries.

Step 4: Find the Stash

Next load the latitude and longitude coordinates (or the waypoint) into your GPS unit. You can venture forth based on this information, or you can decrypt additional clues. These clues are encrypted so they won't spoil someone else's hunt. Deciphering the Chief Muncie clues, for instance, reveals that, "My left hand leads the way." If you want even more clues, you can read the logged visits for the cache.

Finding a tree-trunk geocache.

For caches that involve hiking, once you drive as far as you can, you can load the latitude and longitude of your car into your unit. Label this waypoint "car." (It may also be a good idea to mark this spot on your map.) It's easy to allow your enthusiasm for the find to wipe out your memory of where you parked. Losing your car while visiting Chief Muncie would be nearly impossible, since you'll probably be parked near the statue, but for difficult caches hidden atop mountains or in deep forests, entering your vehicle's waypoint is essential.

Lightposts are common hiding places.

Finding the coordinates on a website and loading them into your GPS unit is easy. Actually finding the cache can be more difficult. Follow the arrow on your GPS unit. As you approach the cache, begin to think like the person who hid it. Look for trails or roads the host may have used to reach the stash. Did she climb the rock wall or take the easier grade of the forest road? Did he stash the cache behind the rock or at the base of the shrub?

Once you get within 25 feet of the cache, you'll want to really turn up your sleuthing skills. You need to remember that the waypoint can be either the location of the cache itself, or a vantage point from which you can spot it. Look for places that are large enough to hide sizeable geocache containers, such as a five-gallon bucket, an ammo box, or a foot-long plastic tube. Stay alert for hiding places like hollow stumps, clumps of cattails, the nooks of boulders, or piles of pine needles. If you are seeking out microcaches in cities, ask yourself, "Where would I hide a small tin?" Your search may have you peeking under park benches, loitering around alleys, or wading through hedges.

Step 5: After You've Found It—Geocache Etiquette

The beauty of geocaching is that it's based on an honor system established when the first cache was stashed by Dave Ulmer:

- Take something from the stash.
- Leave something in the cache.
- Record your visit in the logbook.

Caches typically consist of a waterproof container, a logbook for visitors to sign, and a selection of prizes. Some treasures can be exciting—especially those that capture the local flavor or require you to move a treasure to another cache (see *hitchhiker* in the "Cachionary," chapter 9). While the majority of treasures are of the bargain-bin variety, other finds are more valuable.

Geocachers have stashed toys, tools, batteries (for GPS units), CDs, DVDs, and local souvenirs. Sometimes the location itself is the cache (see virtual cache, page 69). Take a treasure if you like—but if you do, make sure to replace it with one of your own, typically of greater or equal value.

Sometimes the host has stashed a disposable camera. The intent is to have you take a picture of yourself rather than take the camera. Taking photos is, of course, optional, because you may subsequently find yourself posted on the host's website. To help the host of the cache identify you, list the frame in which you are photographed in your logbook entry.

When you're rummaging through your knapsack for an item to exchange, remember that geocaching is an all-ages activity. While a bottle of whiskey may be a treasure for you, it might not be the best item for, say, a Boy Scout geocaching with his troop. Avoid leaving knives, lighters, and fireworks. Also, food should not be left in caches. Savvy squirrels, chipmunks, and bears will usually claim these items before any person ever will—and these critters probably won't make a logbook entry, either!

If you choose not to take an item, just write "TNLN," which stands for "Took nothing, left nothing," into the logbook. Logbook notations are generally simple entries that read like a string of instant messages. They can include your geocaching nickname, the date and time, and what you took and replaced. Some logbooks, however, can be highly entertaining, with recommendations of must-see area attractions, LOL jokes, or even clever short stories (See "Story Cache" in chapter 5).

What your entries in the online logbook should not do, however, is give away the location of the cache. Avoid writing "spoilers" or clues in the logbook or on the cache's web page that could taint someone else's search. Do write things like:

"Cool hiding place! I took a yo-yo and left a harmonica." Don't write: "Awesome sycamore tree. This has to be the biggest one I've ever seen! I took a DVD and left a rubber band before placing the ammo box back in the hollow trunk."

Many geocache hosts leave a logbook for guests to sign. Once you find the cache, record your name, date, what you took from the cache, and what you added for others to find.

British Columbia Cache
N 48° 37.904 • W 123° 31.747
(WGS84)
UTM: 10U E 461015 N 5386654

Be sure to reseal the container and return it to its hiding place, taking care to leave it as you found it. In addition, remember to leave no trace of your visit to the outdoors. Since you've entered your car as a waypoint, you should be able to find your way back.

Once you return to your computer, log on to the cache's web page and post your comments regarding your find—even if you couldn't actually locate the cache. (Posting comments is optional, since you typically have to register on the website.) Why note your failed attempt? This will help the host count the number of visitors and keep track of the cache. Several "no find" entries could indicate that it's missing, the coordinates are incorrect, or it's more difficult than the host intended.

If the cache is there and you just didn't find it the first time, come back the next day after you've studied the clues and other geocachers' comments (know that you'll usually be able to extract a few spoilers from others' comments). Your comments—from "I can't find it!" to "Wahoo! I did it!"—will typically be welcomed by the host and other visitors as good reading, another dramatic chapter in the world of geocaching. Active geocache logs are collections of success stories, hints to the host that the cache needs attention, or praise that the cache was exactly how everyone imagined it would be—an ever-evolving history of the cache. Just remember not to spend all your time reading logs. Get out and find a geocache!

3
GPS Units and Smartphones

In this specialized world we live in, there are GPS units tailored for nearly every activity imaginable. They are used for tracking shipping and trucking companies' cargo and fleets, aeronautical and automobile navigation, surveying, keeping tabs on prison parolees, earth science experiments, military maneuvers, tracking your hunting dog while in the field, guiding anglers to their favorite honey holes, mapping mountain bike and hiking trails, and of course, geocaching—to mention just a few.

While there are many quality GPS units on the market, smartphones are quickly taking over every aspect of our networked lives. Some of these devices are primarily designed as phones but are augmented with GPS capability. While some of these models' accuracy can be questionable at times, it's only a matter of time before the problems are remedied. This is demonstrated by devices like the Garminfone. Garmin has worked out the bugs from its earlier models to give geocachers a solid phone as well as a quality GPS unit in one. More manufacturers will certainly follow suit.

This chapter will provide you with guidelines for purchasing a GPS receiver or smartphone. It will also help you find geocaches posted on the Internet, plug the waypoints into your GPS unit, and actually navigate your way to them.

Purchasing a GPS Receiver or Smartphone

With so many GPS units out there serving so many niche markets, it's best to consider what qualities your GPS unit should have to help you go geocaching. You should also review all of your electronic device needs to see if a GPS-equipped smartphone can effectively integrate your networking and navigation needs.

Factors to consider include size, weight, durability, water resistance, battery life, processing speed, storage capacity, and accuracy. Depending on the quality you choose and the features you want, handheld GPS units can cost from $70 to $600. The old sporting goods truism applies: If you pick the lightest, most durable, most waterproof unit with the fastest processor, the longest-lasting batteries, and the highest level of accuracy, you have probably just selected the most expensive unit on the market.

After you read this chapter, talk with the staff at your favorite outdoor, electronics, or smartphone store to help whittle down the list of features you'll need. You can also review the plethora of online reviews and log on to various forums to talk with other geocachers and learn what equipment they prefer. In the meantime, here's some information to get you started.

Since you are going to be hiking with your GPS unit, you should probably select the lightest unit available. Most handheld units are comparable in weight to smartphones. With continual improvements in technology, there's almost no limit to the number of advanced features that can be packed into these increasingly smaller and lighter units.

Batteries can last as few as six hours or as many as twenty-four. These lives may sound way too short, especially if you are planning a weeklong, backcountry geocaching trek. Remember, though, that on many occasions your GPS unit will only be on a few minutes at a time. Some receivers also have a battery-saving mode. This feature allows the unit to update its position at a slower rate. (Regardless, it's a good idea to have spare batteries on hand.)

GPS receivers typically use alkaline, lithium, or rechargeable batteries. Knowing that batteries are hot commodities, some geocachers leave them behind as treasures you can select—a heartwarming surprise, especially when your power is fading and you discover that you forgot your spare batteries at home.

External power cords can help extend the life of your batteries. These cords can be plugged into electrical outlets at home while you download maps or coordinates into your receiver. The cords can also be plugged into your car's power outlet, fueling your receiver as you drive toward geocaches.

Maryland Cache
N 39° 01.587 • W 76° 59.943
(WGS84)
UTM: 18S E 326956 N 4321613

If your receiver does not come with these accessories, cords and adaptors can be purchased at many electronics stores or online. Just make sure to select accessories that have the same voltage requirements as your receiver.

Consider choosing a receiver that is durable and waterproof—or at least water-resistant—when you make your purchase. Is it going to conk out after one fall on a dirt trail? Short out in a light drizzle? Or will it stay intact after banging 100 yards through class 5 rapids? The terrain in which you will be seeking geocaches can help you decide just how durable and water-resistant your unit should be. If you decide to save some money by purchasing a unit with low water resistance, you can buy waterproof pouches to protect your GPS unit.

Knowing what climate zone you'll be spending most of your time in can also help you with the selection process. All electronic products have upper and lower temperature limits. Estimate how much time you plan on geocaching in the desert during the summer or how many caches you're going to seek during subfreezing temperatures and choose a receiver that best functions in those conditions.

The term "receiver channels" refers to the number of satellites from which the unit can receive information. To effectively locate position, a unit needs to read at least three satellites; four, to calculate position including altitude. Increasing the number of satellites increases the unit's accuracy. Eight channels should be the minimum for any receiver, with most receivers using twelve.

Most receivers have internal antennas. Some have external ones as well. Some handheld GPS units with internal antennas have external antenna interfaces that increase accuracy. These can be used while driving or can be attached to a backpack while hiking to improve accuracy.

Like many display technologies, GPS screens have seen great technological advances. While no-frills models have basic black-and-white displays, most new models have full-color screens, touchscreen capabilities, and can display detailed 3-D maps. Most units have sunlight viewable screens that provide vivid readability in all light conditions. They also have a moving map display that scrolls as you move along.

The trend in smartphone manufacturing is to offer devices that are GPS-compatible. While geocaching is traditionally done with GPS units, it seems that smartphone use amongst geocachers is increasing. It's seemingly only a matter of time before all smartphones are GPS equipped.

While some current models are GPS equipped, the accuracy isn't as good as dedicated GPS units—yet. However, other models, like the Garminfone, have worked out the bugs of their earlier models and now offer geocachers a one-device solution for their phone, network, and GPS needs. It's a fair assessment to say this trend will continue, and there will be a number of high-quality choices on the market soon.

Memory storage should also be considered for your purchase. How many maps can be loaded into your unit? How many waypoints can it store? How fast will the detailed maps be processed? Basic units can store up to twenty routes and one hundred waypoints, and advanced units can store more than 1,000 waypoints. More expensive GPS units have external memory card options, which can greatly enhance storage capacity. Along with such increased storage capacity, units with more megabytes can also download more maps. Some units have their own map database, while others have the capacity to download additional maps.

Many companies offer GPS units specifically designed for geocaching. These units come with preloaded maps, as many as 250,000 geocaches, geocaching games, and more. Many support paperless geocaching, which will allow you to view geocache descriptions, log entries, and more via your unit rather than a printout. (Though this may require purchasing premium membership packages from geocaching websites to take full advantage of the features.)

GPS accuracy has seen great improvement in both the government and private sectors in the years since Selective Availability was turned off. That flip of the switch alone resulted in location accuracy improving from 100 meters to 5 or 10, but many units also employ state-of-the-art Wide Area Augmentation System (WAAS) accuracy to pinpoint locales within 10 feet or less.

Geocachers also have plenty of software and accessories from which to choose. Some companies offer GPS units equipped with two-way radios and peer-to-peer tracking functions that allow fellow geocachers to talk and track each other in the outdoors. A few have digital cameras, which allow you to take geotagged photos. Others have features such as barometric altimeters, flashlights, heart-rate monitors, and more. Others come with bicycle handlebar mounts and wrist straps, which allow you to wear your receiver like a timepiece. Since GPS satellites use atomic clocks, the most accurate clocks in the world, this would be an improvement over most wristwatches. DeLorme, Magellan, and many other GPS-oriented companies also sell software that includes detailed street maps, topographic maps, nautical charts, points of interest, and more.

In closing, buying the right GPS unit or smartphone can be as much fun as finding a geocache. So, review as many as possible before making your final purchase.

For more information on GPS units, check out these manufacturers' websites:
Garmin: www.garmin.com
DeLorme: www.delorme.com
Magellan: www.magellangps.com
Lowrance: www.lowrance.com

GPS Navigation

In the realm of GPS, waypoints are specific locations that you create by entering coordinates from maps, websites, or books into your receiver, or simply by saving your current location into the unit.

A geocache's waypoint or coordinates are listed on its web page. These web pages can in turn be found at host sites like Navicache.com, Geocaching.com, or Buxley's Geocaching Waypoint. The way most host sites are set up, you can type in the zip code, city, or state where you wish to go geocaching and then select which geocaches you would like to visit.

Follow the directions that came with your GPS receiver for loading waypoints and enter the coordinates of the geocache. Now you can start following the arrow on your receiver. You can enter additional waypoints as you go by saving your current location. When two or more waypoints are combined, a route is formed by connecting the locations. For example, when you arrive at the parking lot to begin your hike to the geocache, enter your car as a waypoint (the first being the geocache's waypoint). As you begin walking toward the stash, you can add additional waypoints at critical junctures such as trail intersections, creek crossings, or easily identifiable landmarks like giant redwoods, frog ponds, or hilltop vistas.

If you're seeking a microcache in an urban setting, you'll likely need no more than your GPS receiver and a street map. If the geocache is located in the backcountry, however, it's a good idea to match up the route in your receiver to a topographic map (or vice versa).

Reviewing a topographic map will give you the detailed information you need to find the best trails, fords, and easy grades that bypass cliffs and canyons. It may not be the quickest route as the crow flies, but it will be the most efficient path to the hidden prize. Once you've mapped your route, use either a latitude/longitude ruler or Universal Transverse Mercator (UTM) reader to determine the waypoints along your route. Latitude/longitude and UTM references are located in the margins of topographic maps.

Now load the route into your GPS unit. Make sure the map and your receiver are using the same map datum. WGS84—the World Geodetic System of 1984—is the GPS mapping standard. But many maps in North America use NAD27—North American Datum 1927. And some countries use different datums altogether.

Give the waypoints a feature name, a numerical sequence name, or a combination of the two. For example, your first waypoint can be called truck or simply one. If the second waypoint is Salamander Pond, you can call it salpon or salama2. If your route has more waypoints than will fit into your receiver's routes, break the trip into two separate routes and overlap the ending waypoints. Since most receivers have a route-reversal feature, you'll just need to reverse the route to return to your vehicle.

Bring along the topographic map and your written route and place them in a plastic bag. When you arrive at the trailhead, pull out your map and your GPS unit and check to see whether everything matches up and is making sense. Visualizing your map will help you navigate and gauge the map's scale. Orient your map by laying it on a flat, nonmetallic surface so the compass directions on the map correspond with those in the field. (Metal, such as a car hood, can throw off compass readings.) Look at the hills and see how these are symbolized by compressed contour lines on the map; spot the trail snaking down a ravine separating two ridges and how the map has it traced through a V in the contour lines; look at the small stream and see that the map denotes this as a dashed blue line.

Now turn to distance: See how far away all these features are and compare this with how it's measured on the map. Lay your compass on the map to see the exact position, in terms of degrees, of these features. Then take a bearing at the trailhead and see how this compares with the direction your GPS receiver is telling you to go.

As you walk, follow the arrow on your GPS unit and track your progress with your receiver and on the map to note how long it takes to reach distinct features. This will help you establish a timetable for your return trip, and it will also help you bask in all the wonderful scenery on the way to the geocache.

Compare your progress across the map with the route stored in your GPS receiver. Tracking features are great for mapping, but they drain power quickly. To save even more battery life, see if your receiver has a power-saver mode. This setting allows your unit to receive signals and plot locations at a slower-than-normal rate, ultimately allowing the power to siphon off at a slower rate. It's also a good idea to recharge your battery while you drive by using a power cord adaptor that plugs into your car's power outlet.

If you lose signal strength while driving, try moving the unit to different places inside the car. In some cases, you may find that the dashboard is not the best place for reception. Also, an external antenna interface can be used to help boost signal strength while driving.

One final battery-saving tip: Cold weather tends to sap the life from batteries. So keep your receiver in a warm pocket whenever you can. (Roaming out of service

Map-reading skills are still essential in the backcountry. A map and compass can help you find the best route and serve as a backup if your GPS unit quits working.

can also drain your smartphone, so keep an eye on battery levels when wandering the backwoods.)

Remember that GPS units, no matter how accurate they become, are not a substitute for map and compass skills. Studying maps and plotting routes with a compass, when combined with GPS navigation, will make you a savvy, directionally competent geocacher.

4
Creating Caches

Now that you've found a few caches and have seen how others have done it, why not try your hand at stashing a cache yourself? Just as there is no fee for geocaching, there is no charge for placing geocaches and posting them to an Internet site.

Hiding caches out of sight protects them from geomuggles.

The Hiding Spot

First you need to pick a place for your cache. Will it be hidden in a dense forest? Or will it be a microcache concealed beneath a park bench? Many geocachers play the game for the joy of the find and to discover beautiful places where they have never been before. So try to pick a spot that's worth visiting—perhaps a place with a pristine vista or a resting place where the city's ducks and geese gather at sunset.

Whether your cache is on private or public land, you need to ask permission from the landowner or the property manager before placing it. Private property owners should be informed that the cache could potentially have many guests. In the same vein, geocachers should be made aware that even though there may be NO TRESPASSING signs posted, they are welcome to visit the cache. Once you have permission, it's recommended that you include this information in your cache and that you also post this permission with your cache listing on the web.

Local and national parks hold great potential for geocachers, but you must know their rules. By working with park rangers, you can learn about what areas are dangerous or off-limits to hikers and geocachers. You will also learn about sensitive ecological areas that rangers are trying to protect. On the other side of the coin, you can then help educate them on geocaching. Once they learn that geocachers are responsible, environmentally conscious folk with a respect for zero-impact principles, local park rangers will usually welcome the opportunity to have more visitors.

To honor your part of the relationship, you need to select a cache location that does not jeopardize the natural setting or require visitors to dig to find it. Take the time to choose a place that hides your cache but does not demand that visitors bushwhack, stomp, or trample their way to find it.

The National Park Service reviews geocaching on a case-by-case basis. NPS officials have also indicated

Finding the cannon was easy. Finding where the cache was hidden took some time.

that they are in favor of virtual caches—those where the treasure is simply the location rather than a bucketful of booty. Working with geocachers, they could suggest visually enticing locations or suggest waypoints that are part of tours that highlight the parks' beauty. For more information on the National Park Service, log on to www .nps.gov.

The Treasure

Now that you've carefully selected a location, it's time to choose a container. First and foremost, it should be waterproof. It should be rugged, too. For full-size caches, five-gallon buckets with lids, old ammunition boxes, and plastic kitchen containers are commonly used. For microcaches—tiny caches commonly hidden by geo-cachers in urban settings—cagey cachers have affixed Altoids tins with magnets to metal surfaces or stashed tubes wrapped with camouflage tape in hedgerows. (There are even nanocaches out there that are as small as pencil erasers.)

Whether your cache is micro or macro, the word "geo-cache" should be clearly marked on your container, and a geocaching letter should accompany your cache. Varia-tions on this letter can be downloaded from Geocaching. com, Navicache.com, or brillig.com/geocaching—or see the sample letter on pages 43 and 44. Marking the con-tainer and including the letter accomplishes two tasks.

Magnetic holders make for well-hidden caches.

First, if a neophyte (insiders call them geomuggles) accidentally stumbles upon it, your cache will immediately be associated with the worldwide treasure-hunting game. Seeing that it is a game rather than forgotten loot will hopefully keep the geomuggle from pillaging it (thus maintaining geomuggles' reputation as harmless, peaceloving folks). Just as important, it also tells people you have not planted something illegal such as a bomb or a stash of drugs (a sad, but necessary statement).

One way to reduce the number of accidental finds is to pick a hiding place that is not out in the open. Even

What should you stash?
Geocaching treasures can include
dollar-store trinkets, toys, tools,
batteries, CDs, and DVDs.

for easy caches, it's best not to make them so easy that anyone walking past can spot them.

Your cache, at the very least, should have a logbook for visitors to sign. This can be a full-size, spiral-bound notebook or (for a microcache) a small pad of paper. You can start the log by including your geocaching nickname, date, time, and possibly some comments as to why you chose this great place for your cache. A pen and pencil should accompany your notebook for visitors to add their entries.

You can choose to offer simply the location as your geocache—a virtual cache—and leave only a logbook, or

Argentina Cache
N 11° 08.969 • W 063° 54.286
(WGS84)
UTM: 20P E 401206 N 1232659

you can offer a selection of prizes. In Dave Ulmer's inaugural cache, as you'll recall, he left some cash, videos, books, software, and a slingshot. The range of gifts is up to you. Treasures can include toys, tools, batteries (for GPS units), CDs, DVDs, and local souvenirs. Even though your container is waterproof, it's a good idea to stow your treasures in sealed plastic bags.

Hitchhikers—items placed in a cache that are designated to travel to other caches—are another treasure option. Some come with specific instructions: "Travel westbound," for instance, or simply "Take me to as much of the world as possible." The hitchhikers' travels can be documented in a logbook or on their accompanying web pages. Travel bugs are hitchhikers whose progress can be monitored on Geocaching.com.

It's worth reemphasizing here that since geocaching is an all-ages activity, it's wise to leave G-rated items—prizes that are not offensive, illegal, or dangerous. Avoid leaving items such as alcohol, knives, lighters, and fireworks. Also, food should not be left in caches. As mentioned earlier,

SAMPLE GEOCACHE LETTER

Geocache Site—Please Read

Congratulations! You've found it!

This container was placed here as part of a worldwide GPS stash hunt also known as geocaching.

GPS users hide treasure, like this container, and publish the coordinates via the Internet so other GPS users can find it. The only rules are: If you take something from the cache, you must leave something in exchange, and you must write about your visit in the logbook.

If you found this container by accident:

Great! You are welcome to join us! Here's all we ask:

- Do not move or vandalize the container.
- Do not remove this notice from the container.
- Do not remove all of the contents.
- Do not take the disposable camera—but you're welcome to take a picture of yourself and log the frame number in the logbook.
- If you wish, take something. But please leave something of your own for others and write about your visit in the logbook.

To learn more about this activity, log on to any of these websites for more information:

www.geocaching.com

www.navicache.com

www.brillig.com/geocaching

Geocaching is open to everyone with a GPS unit and a sense of adventure. There are similar sites all over the world.

If this container needs to be moved for any reason, please let us know. We apologize, and we will be happy to remove it.

Cache Name: _____

Coordinates: _____

Placed By: _____

E-Mail: _____

_____

the local wildlife will usually be the FTF (first to find) these items—and they rarely bother signing the logbook.

Some hosts stash disposable cameras, with the intent being to have guests take pictures of themselves. Once the film is used, you can create an Internet logbook of all of the guests. To help match geocachers' photos to their names, ask them to list the frame number next to their logbook entry.

Making It Public

Now that you have properly prepared your cache, choose a website to share it with the world. Choose from one of the sites listed in chapter 8. Most of the sites have basic guidelines that must be met before they will accept your listing. In general, you'll need to register on the site using your geocaching nickname, and you'll need to provide:

- A name for the cache.
- Its coordinates.
- The type of cache (micro, virtual, what have you).
- The date it was placed.
- The state and country where it's located.
- A difficulty rating for the find, and for the terrain.
- Any comments, such as a short explanation of what makes this location special.

Make sure your coordinates are correct. While standing at your site, check your receiver to make sure it has good reception before recording the waypoint. As an added precaution, walk away from the site and return to double-check your reading. Along with a general rating, you may want to consider rating your geocache site's level of handicapped accessibility.

Provide as much information about your cache without giving away its location. On Navicache.com, geocache hosts are asked to provide comments regarding the availability of water, restrooms, and parking; whether the cache is wheelchair accessible; and if pets are allowed. Detailed clues and spoilers can be included, but they are encrypted so they won't spoil the experience for someone who wants more of a challenge.

Placing your cache and posting it to a website obligates you to maintain the cache. This means that you have to check in on it on a regular basis. Checking in on your cache can be a blend of actual and virtual visits on its web page. Perusing the comments on the web page logbook can offer clues to the cache's condition. If it's in disrepair, visitors will typically note this when they post their comments.

If your cache becomes drenched, it's up to you to replace the logbook, check the seal on your container, and try to ensure it stays dry in the future. Once it's fixed, log your maintenance efforts to your cache's web page log. If the website managers notice that you aren't tending your site, they will probably archive it (that is, delete it from their listings).

Some caring geocachers have even taken to adopting abandoned geocaches. At Geocaching.com, they list caches in need of adoption. Because let's face it, a happy cache is a tended cache.

5
Geo-Games

Through the ages we humans have incorporated most of our tools and inventions into play. Spears once hurled at woolly mammoths have evolved into javelins heaved in the Olympics; no sooner were cars rolling off Ford's assembly line than they were racing around banked oval tracks; and compasses, once reserved for world exploration, are now used for orienteering and adventure races.

GPS technology, developed and guarded by the military, is not being left out of this trend. Just hours after the jamming signal was switched off, Dave Ulmer set out the first geocache. And while traditional geocaching continues to flourish, so do the spin-offs.

While geocaching has generated all kinds of activities in its own right, there are a number of other games that influenced its creation, and still others that are similar in nature. Some games have been around for many years; others are rooted in childhood pastimes, such as tag and huckle-buckle-beanstalk; still others have been uncorked from the imaginations of geocaching enthusiasts.

Once you've mastered the basics of geocaching, you can take the game and your newfound treasure-hunting skills to a whole new level. This chapter will introduce you to many different "geo-games." Many involve collecting one specific type of treasure as part of an ongoing game or competition. Others are simply a good excuse to get you outdoors hiking or running—or honing your GPS, map, and compass skills. If you don't see a game you'd like to play, make up your own and share it with as many people as you'd like.

Are U Nuts?

The folks in Utah, it seems, are nuts about geocaching. They're so enthusiastic, in fact, that they hide nuts in their caches.

Geocachers in the Beehive State find the nuts in one cache, move them to another cache within the state, and collect points for each nutty transaction. Sometimes these games can get fairly competitive, so the game's creator says, "Thanks for playing the nut game. Please play nicely." **For more information, visit the Utah Association of Geocachers (UTAG):** www.utahgeocachers.com

Armchair Treasure Hunting

Move over, armchair quarterbacks; here come the armchair treasure hunters. The concept was inspired by the 1979 book *Masquerade,* which held cryptic clues on the whereabouts of a golden bunny encrusted with jewels.

While many clues for these hunts come from books, other hunts drop hints via websites, jigsaw-puzzle pieces, audiotapes, playing cards, letters, photographs, and maps. Some treasures are hidden on the Internet, while other bounty is actually buried underground. Once hunters have an inkling of where such buried treasure is hidden, armchair potatoes become treasure seekers to find where X marks the spot.

Clubs like the Armchair Treasure Hunt Club keep tabs on hunts around the world. This particular group was founded in 1992 by English author Dan James. Taking a cue from *Masquerade,* he published a complex treasure hunt that sent people seeking a buried bronze statuette. The hunt, "A Timeless Moral," was so difficult that the statuette remained buried for three years. Fortunately, not all armchair treasure hunts are that difficult. One, consisting of three photos of landmarks and a brief explanation, took only six hours to solve.

Some hunts are restricted solely to the Internet. By sleuthing through cyberspace, web-surfing Sherlocks can solve mysteries without leaving the comfort of their mouse pads.

For more information, check out: www.treasureclub.net

Benchmark Hunting

When the National Geodetic Survey (NGS) plotted its way across the United States, it left many permanent markers to aid its efforts in land surveying, civil engineering, and mapping. Luckily for the survey, the locations for the more than 700,000 markers are saved in a database.

Luckily for geocaching enthusiasts, the database is available to the public at www.ngs.noaa.gov/, thus providing another endless list of treasure sites. By using your GPS unit and written directions provided by the NGS, you can seek out NGS survey markers and other natural and human-made features used in surveying. In many cases you'll be able to find the markers solely from the NGS directions. Lists of benchmarks, a photo gallery, and benchmark-hunting etiquette can be found at www.geocaching.com.

Many of the markers are made of brass or aluminum attached to a concrete post. Others may simply be a mountain peak, water tower, smokestack, church spire, or radio tower. While some may be challenging to find, others may be so obvious that you have been walking past them for years.

To seek benchmarks by state:
www.ngs.noaa.gov/cgi-bin/ds_desig.prl

To search by a marker's permanent identifier number (PID):
www.ngs.noaa.gov/cgi-bin/ds_radius.prl

To be a part of a benchmark-seeking community:
www.geocaching.com/mark

Bingocaching

Geocaching is helping to solve an age-old riddle: If you shout "Bingo!" in the woods, but no one is around to hear it, do you make a sound? Forget silly puns and remember that bingocaching is more fun played in the great outdoors than in smoky American Legion halls.

For quick games, game boards can be passed out at an event or downloaded from the sponsor club's website before the event (assuming that club members have planned ahead). Numbered tokens are stashed in caches that are relatively close together. The first person to find the necessary tokens can call in "Bingo!" to a designated game coordinator via two-way radio or cell phone.

For longer games, tokens can be spread around a city, county, or state. Since longer games are played at a more leisurely pace, players can post their finds to the bingo host's website. This will help you keep tabs on other players' progress as well.

CacheAcrossAmerica

In the spirit of sea-to-shining-sea, and taking a cue from Hands Across America, a geocaching enthusiast known as Scout created CacheAcrossAmerica in June 2001, which linked a series of caches from coast to coast.

While Scout's game has already concluded (it took until July 31, 2002!), the game can certainly be played again. A chain is started when someone sets out or finds

He didn't know where the cache was either.

a cache within 100 meters of the Atlantic or the Pacific Ocean. The chain is extended by someone who finds or places another cache within 100 miles of the previous cache. It is finished when someone finds the final cache within 100 meters of the opposite shore. A chain can also meet in the middle. Two separate chains, one starting on the East Coast and another beginning on the west, can be connected and finished by someone placing a cache within 100 miles of two separate chains.

For more information on CacheAcrossAmerica:
groups.yahoo.com/group/CacheAcrossAmerica

Chicken

This is a simple game that can be used to pass the time while hiking or geocaching—especially with children. At the beginning of the hike, record the location of the trailhead in your GPS unit. Now pick a distance—say, 1 mile.

The goal of the game is to guess when you reach that distance. Anyone in the group can call out "stop" whenever he thinks the distance has been reached. You can score the game however you'd like. For example, if the distance is over 1 mile, the caller wins. If it's under, the other person wins.

Another variation would be to call out the exact distance. If someone stops at the right distance, you can reward her with a prize.

This game and others are listed at:
www.gpsgames.org

Cloo

Geocachers in Utah have taken the old board game favorite Clue and adapted it to geocaching. "Cloo," adapted by geocaching enthusiast SirGerald, has GPS-toting Sherlock wannabes scouring the Beehive State to solve murder mysteries.

Like the board game, Cloo requires potential puzzle solvers to find the correct suspect, weapon, and location. Rather than using stodgy characters like Colonel Mustard and tired weapons like the candlestick, SirGerald came up with suspects like Jerry Cherry, Polly Pine, and Maggie Maple and weapons such as arsenic-laced tea, a chain saw, and a really big stick. Players collect clues at various caches and use them to complete a URL that holds the correct answer.

For detailed instructions on Cloo and to find out where the next round is being played, go to:

www.utahgeocachers.com

County Highpointers

From the summit of Mount McKinley to the swamps of Louisiana, County Highpointers are visiting every county highpoint in the United States.

A list of the 3,141 county highpoints and their coordinates can be found at www.cohp.org. At this site you can also find the locale of America's toughest county summits—Alaska notwithstanding. (According to the site, Alaska's counties are in a class by themselves.) You can also see what county highpoints have yet to be summited.

You can plan conquests of first ascents, choose a role model for your county highpoint quests (see "County Highpoint King and Queen"), track how many peaks other highpointers have bagged, and learn about a two-fer (a pair of adjacent counties sharing a highpoint) and a three-fer (three counties sharing an apex). You can also find the counties with the best names for their highpoints, such as Ebright Azimuth (New Castle, Delaware), Hoosier Hill (Wayne, Indiana), Pickles Butte (Canyon, Idaho), and Love's Knob (Barren, Kentucky).

For all the information you need:

www.cohp.org

The Degree Confluence Project

The goal of this game, according to the website www .confluence.org, is to "visit each of the latitude and longitude integer degree intersections in the world, and to take pictures at each location." That simple request has fielded more than 90,000—and counting—photographs of such intersections around the world.

To begin, you need to create an account on the host's website. Once you've registered, select a confluence to visit—there is one within 49 miles of any locale—and submit a plan for your trip. The webmaster will be able to tell you if there are any other plans being processed regarding the confluence you wish to visit. The first person to the confluence, like the race to the North Pole, will be the person credited with the first find. (Though both will be credited for the visit.)

To receive credit, you will be asked to get within 100 meters of the confluence, document the visit with two to five digital photos, and write a short description of what is there. Getting this close is fairly easy if you have a GPS unit, more challenging if you're using a map and compass. **For more information:** www.confluence.org

Event Cache

The subtitle to this game should be, "Where geocachers meet." Even though it sounds like a GPS-adapted singles mixer, dating is not usually involved—although if dinner plans evolve from bringing together like-minded people, so be it.

A specific date, time, and coordinates are posted on a website, and the gathering becomes the cache. Participants can then log their thoughts and post pictures of the event, of the people they meet, and of the location they visited. Once the geoparty has finished, the cache is archived and deleted from the Internet.

Event caches can be found at individual geocaching clubs' websites or at:
www.geocaching.com
www.navicache.com

Garmin Games

Garmin International, Inc., has created many games specifically for its GPS units. The basic premise of each is that the GPS units display a game board that in actuality represents an outdoor playing field. As players run around the field, their action is tracked via their GPS units.

Geko Smak is the GPS version of Whac-A-Mole. When a lizard pops up on your GPS screen, you must run to the location and whack it by pressing your ok button before the lizard disappears from the display. As the game progresses, the lizards appear quicker and farther away, leaving players laughing and breathless.

Memory Race has gamers match different symbols inside treasure chests within a grid system. As players run outside, their path is tracked and their treasures are counted on the grid displayed on the screen.

Nibbons is a navigational strategy game. Players need to travel to sequential markers without crossing their own tracks. If they do, they have to start over.

Virtual Maze has players navigate a labyrinth in search of markers. The goal is to collect all the virtual flags in the least amount of time. Gamers can choose from three difficulty levels and three sizes of mazes. Each maze is randomly generated and can be synchronized with others who have Geko GPS units.

For more information: www.garmin.com

Geodashing

This game transforms the entire planet into a playing field. Geodashing's creator, geocaching enthusiast Scout, uses a computer program to randomly select a large set of waypoints or dashpoints, posts them to www.gpsgames.org, and gives players or teams one month to find them. The true randomness of the program scatters these points from suburban streets to wilderness plateaus.

You can compete individually or as a team of up to five players to visit as many dashpoints as possible. The first to visit a dashpoint gets three points; second place gets two points; every other visitor gets one point. To document your visit, you must submit a description of the point. Photographs are helpful but not required. The team or individual with the most points wins. The competition is friendly, and teamwork is strongly encouraged. New games are created each month.

For more information: www.gpsgames.org

Geodashing Golf

Is it necessary to scream, "Fore!" when a virtual golf ball is about to hit someone? Since geogolf doesn't involve errant golf balls, we may never know. What we do know is that that this game involves players navigating eighteen randomly placed waypoints (nine in a short game). Your score is determined by how close you can get to each of the waypoints. The closer you get, the lower your score, with the lowest score being the winner.

For more information: www.gpsgames.org

GeosportZ

Also known as GZ, this Australian-inspired game is based on the modern Olympics. The complete game will have participants competing in equestrian, marathon, kayaking, sailing, triathlon, and more.

For more details, visit: www.gpsgames.com

Geoteaming

Geocaching has gone corporate. The next time your company needs a team-building exercise, why not recommend something you already enjoy doing? To paraphrase an R.E.M. song, it sure beats walking on coals to improve your business acumen.

Geocaching.com and PlayTime, Inc., created Geoteaming to enhance corporate team building with a GPS twist. Teams are given GPS units with preprogrammed coordinates to find. At these waypoints, participants must locate hidden prizes or perform a team challenge. According to the website, these challenges can take the form of finding a puzzle piece, scaling a wall, or creating a raft to reach the next location.

With a facilitator observing your team's progress, you can identify your group's strengths and weaknesses. You and your coworkers should also improve communications with each other, work more efficiently together, and pinpoint what you need to reach the next level.

For more information:

www.geocaching.com/geoteaming

Hide-and-Seek

Instead of looking for caches, you are looking for people. The simplified version has a single person hiding at a specified location or waypoint. Seekers can go looking for the person and the quickest way to the waypoint. To increase the difficulty, have seekers go through a series of clue caches before finding the person or people.

Jeep 4x4 Geocaching Challenge

To roll out its latest model, Jeep set up its 4x4 geocaching challenge. The carmaker released 8,000 Jeep travel-bugs with the grand prize winners netting a new Jeep. **For more details, visit:** http://jeep.geocaching.com/

Just 4 Openers

Here's another Utah-based game that can be found at www.utahgeocachers.com. The game begins as twenty-three colored bottle openers are hidden in caches around Utah. Just 4 Openers is similar to the nut game in that finders of the openers are charged with moving the colorful finds to another cache rather than keeping them. The goal is to collect enough colored openers to complete a rainbow.

Participants can track everyone's progress on the Cachunuts website. Once you collect six colors, you are given the coordinates of a special "cache at the end of the rainbow." Did someone say pot of gold?

For more information: www.utahgeocachers.com

Letterboxing

Like geocaching, letterboxing involves looking for water-proof boxes of treasure. The difference is that you are exchanging stamps rather than prizes, and you are following clues and coordinates rather than plugging in a waypoint into your GPS receiver. In many cases, too, the clues to a letterbox are more convoluted than a simple waypoint.

Letterboxing's roots can be traced to England, when someone left a calling card in a bottle on the moors of Dartmoor, according to the Letterboxing in America Internet site. In North America the spark for letterboxing came from a 1998 article in *Smithsonian Magazine* on the Dartmoor phenomenon. The sport has since evolved worldwide and has sent droves of logbook-toting seekers into the thickets questing for coveted rubber stamps.

Some clues can be found at www.letterboxing.org, or they might pass via word of mouth. Some clues lead straight to a letterbox. Once you find one, you stamp the letterbox's logbook with your personal stamp, then stamp your logbook with the letterbox's stamp. Participants are encouraged to adopt unique personal stamps rather than common store-bought types. It should be carved by you or, at least, customized to reflect your personality.

Some letterboxes require you to solve a riddle or puzzle, or interpret a poem, before the coveted stamp can be found and added to your logbook. Like geocaching, letterboxing is limited only by your own creativity.

You can also set out your own letterbox. First, find an ideal location (one where it's legal to leave a letterbox). Carve a unique stamp and hide it with a logbook and other goodies, if you'd like, in a sturdy waterproof box. List your clues at a site like Letterboxing in America or create your own.

For more details, check out the books *The Letterboxer's Companion* (FalconGuides) or *Letterboxing,* or log on to:
www.letterboxing.org

Letterbox Hybrid

While letterboxing and geocaching are separate activities, some outdoor treasure-hunting enthusiasts are blending the two. At some hidden—dare we say it—"lettercaches" or "geoboxes," finders have a choice. They can log the find as a geocache and select a prize; mark it as a letterbox and perform the ritual of exchanging stamps; or both.

Maze

If finding your way through mazes featured in magazines or newspapers excites you, imagine navigating (or creating) a maze spanning several acres.

Using a road or trail map, create a maze as clear or as convoluted as you like. Record the waypoints of every intersection by noting its coordinates on a piece of paper along with those of all neighboring intersections. For example, four-way intersections will list four neighboring intersections—four choices of direction—while corners would list two neighboring intersections, or two choices of direction.

Players are given the entrance coordinates and are instructed to look for the paper placed in a waterproof packet to decide where to go to next. The goal, of course, is to find the end of the maze.

This game and others are listed at:

www.gpsgames.org

Microcaching

In urban areas such as New York, microcaches made from 35mm film containers or Altoids boxes have been attached to the bottom of park benches or other metal surfaces with magnets. Since there's not much room for prizes, geocachers will have to be satisfied with simply a logbook entry.

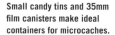
Small candy tins and 35mm film canisters make ideal containers for microcaches.

Minute War

Minute War's founder, geocaching enthusiast Scout, created this game as a global variation on Capture the Flag. Instead of playing in your backyard, you will be using the world as your playing field and navigating it with your GPS unit.

This game is not a quick one, either, as the name may imply. In this instance minute refers to a 60-by-60-mile square or one minute of longitude by one minute of latitude. Degree components are ignored completely. For example, if the game lists a square with coordinates 10 by 10 (this simplified explanation does not use actual coordinates), any square with these minute coordinates represents a single square, regardless of whether it's in the United States or the United Kingdom.

Simplified, Minute War places a neutral flag—virtual rather than actual—inside each designated square, selected by a random computer program. Neutral flags are captured when your team gets within 100 meters of the flag. Like Capture the Flag, Minute War offers ways for you to capture other teams' flags as well. The team with the most flags or the most points—depending on the scoring system—wins.

Detailed copies of the rules, instructions on how to join a team, and other pertinent information can be found at:

www.gpsgames.org

Moving Cache Game

This purpose of this game, which is from the Land Down Under, is to see how far your cache can move during a prescribed time period.

For more information, visit:

www.cachinggames.com.

Multicaches

Multiple caches or multicaches, as the name implies, have more than one cache. Typically, the first cache holds hints to find the second, the second has hints to the third, and so on, for as long as the multicache stasher desires. There can be many variations on this game.

Orienteering

This venerable sport blending map and compass skills with cross-country running began in Sweden in the 1920s. Often called "running with cunning" or "running while playing chess," orienteering rewards the competitor who is swift and savvy.

In Scandinavia orienteering is a national pastime, and meets can draw as many as 17,000 participants. A typical competition involves competitors finding fifteen sequential control points. The winner must find all the control points—red and white prisms hidden in the woods—in the least amount of time.

Skilled competitors study their maps, note the locations of the control points, and visualize the fastest route. And as you can imagine, the quickest route is rarely a straight line.

Many meet organizers offer a category for those who wish to participate in a noncompetitive manner. In orienteering speak, you'll be known as a wayfarer or a map-walker.

For more information, check out:
www.orienteering.org

Poker Run

Three-card poker has been used in everything from church scavenger hunts to offshore boat racing. So it's logical that it be adapted to geocaching. Cards can be stashed in caches with the coordinates posted on a website or given out to players on the day of the event. For single-day events, caches are relatively close together so players can grab three or more cards in a short amount of time. For longer events, cards can be scattered across an entire state; these games can take a month to play.

Project APE

Hollywood didn't wait long to jump into geocaching. To coincide with its 2001 release *Planet of the Apes,* 20th Century-Fox created "Project APE" (Alternative Primate Evolution) and used the geocaching event as a marketing ploy to promote the remake. In all they set up twelve movie-related caches and opened the door to a brandnew avenue for marketers worldwide.

Although the caches have been archived, information on the project can be found at:
www.projectape.com/index.asp

Story Cache

This creative spin-off requires geocachers to have knowledge of latitude, longitude, and literacy. The owner of the cache begins a story—perhaps with a fairy-tale lead ("Once upon a time"), Snoopy's classic ("It was a dark and stormy night"), or something not so corny. Visitors are then asked to do their best Mark Twain impersonation and move the story along. Stories can be based on a theme, can help unravel a mystery, could consist of a collection of poems describing the waypoint, or could be merely a collection of loosely connected thoughts. But maybe, just maybe, a decent short story or even a novel will evolve from this group-writing process. (Kind of reminds you of that old monkeys-in-a-roomful-of-typewriters experiment, doesn't it?)

The owner of the cache can leave the logbook in its paper form, to be read only by visitors, or the multiwriter manuscript could be transcribed and posted to a website.

Stampin' Fools Game

This Utah-based game is a blend of Are U Nuts and letter-boxing. Geocachers must seek out rubber stamps hidden about the Beehive State, add the stamps to their notebook, and log their finds at www.utahgeocachers.com.

More than forty stamps are hidden, each worth five points—except for the crown stamp, which is worth ten—and participants can keep track of the points leaders via the Cachunuts website.

For more information:
www.utahgeocachers.com

Tag

Since some GPS units can interact with each other through peer-to-peer functions, geocachers can now play a high-tech version of "Tag."

The person who is "it" can search for someone to tag via his GPS unit. Once the baton (or sticker, or card, or T-shirt, or whatever to indicate who is "it") is passed, the new person can look for someone else to tag. This can be played on city streets on in-line skates, on mountain bikes in the woods, or while running in someone's big backyard.

Virtual Cache

To play loosely with the language, a virtual cache is a trek to visitational reality. The cache, Grasshopper, is the location itself. Most virtual caches, however, are not coordinates just for coordinates' sake. Virtual caches may not have a five-gallon bucket full of prizes, but the pristine view, the soothing rapids, or the sand dunes at sunset should be rewarding enough to bring a smile to a geocacher's face.

Volksmarching

A form of volkssports—German for "people's sports"— volksmarching is a noncompetitive activity that involves hiking or walking a sanctioned trail or route and receiving credit for your effort.

The governing body, the Internationaler Volkssport-verband, has two logbooks that volksmarchers can use to track their accomplishments: an event book and a distance book. Participants earn pins, patches, T-shirts, mugs, and certificates after ten, thirty, and fifty sanctioned events or after walking 500 kilometers (or more) on sanctioned routes. Many participants keep both books so they can track how many events they have entered and the number of kilometers they have covered.

For more information, check out:

Internationaler Volkssportverband at www.ivv-web.org

American Volkssports Association at www.ava.org

Web-Cam Cache (or Cache Cams)

Rather than take a picture with your GPS unit or smartphone, why not allow the cache to do the work for you? At these caches web cams are ready and waiting to take a picture of you during your visit.

You'll need some help, however, to save your picture while you stand in front of the camera. Call a friend and have her go to the web cam's accompanying Internet site, then save the picture while you ham it up in front of the lens. Once the picture is saved, post your cache cam shot to the website.

Film canisters are common geocache containers.

6

Backcountry Safety and Outdoor Etiquette

Before trekking into the outdoors, heed the Boy Scouts' motto: Be prepared. This means knowing how your body will perform, being ready for what Mother Nature will dole out, and making sure all your equipment is in good working order. It's also recommended that you go geocaching with a friend and to leave a note telling people where you are going, when you left, and what time you will return.

Some Preparedness Guidelines

Only you know your own level of fitness. So pick geocaches that satisfy whatever goals you may have set for your outing and don't exceed your limits. Do you want to take a leisurely stroll on groomed fire roads to a cache that's easy to spot? Or do you want to be challenged with both rugged terrain and a well-camouflaged cache? To get an idea of what's in store for a particular cache, check out the difficulty ratings. Most geocache Internet postings rate both the terrain and how well the cache is hidden. Some caches even list handicapped accessibility.

Alabama Cache
N 33° 44.217 • W 087° 04.535 (WGS84)
UTM: 16S E 492999 N 3732993

Don't forget to peruse the Internet logbook and the visitors' comments. Are there comments like "drove right to the spot" or "the most difficult rappel I have ever made"? One caveat about reading logbooks, though: They may contain spoilers or clues to the cache's location.

If you want to gain insight into the location without spotting revelations of where exactly the cache is stashed, study the area's topographic map. Are there easy-grade trails that lead to the waypoint? Or are there plenty of compressed contour lines indicating steep ravines or sheer walls between you and the cache?

Talking with rangers or landowners will also reveal information about the area's flora and fauna. They can point out trails that are more scenic than others and must-see vistas, as well as danger areas such as rockslide-prone inclines, fast-running streams, or areas of poison ivy or stinging nettles. They can also tell you about any poisonous snakes, scorpions, and spiders and offer alternate routes that avoid pastures laden with ticks or areas notorious for dive-bombing blackflies.

A quick check of the local weather forecast will also help you prepare for an outing. If you don't trust your television meteorologist, log on to www.weather.com just before your excursion. While long-range forecasting is equal parts guesswork and fact, checking the weather an hour before you leave typically provides a more trust-worthy guide. Along with giving you an idea of what to wear, the forecast will also tell you how much impact you'll likely leave on the way. If finding a cache means traipsing a large group down a muddy trail, it may be best to seek another cache or choose another activity for the day.

Clothing for Geocaching

Choosing the appropriate clothes will also make your geocaching experiences more enjoyable. Select gar-ments that will protect against weather, terrain, bugs, and poisonous plants such as poison ivy or stinging nettles. Pants, shorts, and shirts should be made from high-tech outdoor fabric, wool, or polyester—materials that will aid in regulating body heat and moisture in warm or cold weather. Regardless of the temperature, avoid wear-ing clothes made from cotton. After a long hike, cotton clings to your body like a wet towel, keeping moisture close to your skin.

Short-sleeved shirts are fine, but long-sleeved shirts have the advantage of offering additional protection from sunburn, bug bites, and poisonous plants.

Sandals may be comfortable, but they leave you prone to twisted ankles and stubbed toes. Hiking boots and trail-running shoes are durable and designed to protect you from foot and ankle injuries. If there is a chance—even a slim one—the weather could change during your outing, throw a fleece vest and rain gear into your fanny pack or day pack. A fleece vest doesn't take up much space, but is worth its weight for the amount of body heat it can help you save. Rain gear can help stave off the nuisance of a summer downpour or save your life when a cold front blitzes in accompanied by near-freezing drizzle.

Other items to stow for geocaching adventures include bug spray, sunglasses (these offer UV protection, guard your eyes from errant twigs and bugs, and allow you to look cool), and a hat for both sun and bug protection. The old multipurpose bandanna can be worn around your neck to protect that vulnerable area from bug bites and sunburn, dunked in a cool stream and dabbled on your forehead, or serve as a tourniquet or part of a splint.

Food for Geocaching

The right food and drink can also enhance your outing. Water, of course, is essential. Short hikes may call for

Bring along foodstuffs, such as PB&J, granola bars, and water, to stay hydrated and well-fueled during your treasure hunt.

no more than a small water bottle. But longer ones may necessitate a backpack hydration system such as a CamelBak. Many backpack systems, like those used by adventure racers, also double as backpacks—great for stowing extra clothes, maps, batteries, exchange items, and food. If running out of water is a concern, consider taking water purification tablets so you can refill your supplies from streams or lakes. Whether you're taking a short hike or a long one, always bring more water than you'll need. Just as you can bank on the certainty of death and taxes, you can count on running out of water—or having to resupply a buddy who has run out.

A GEOCACHING CHECKLIST

- GPS unit
- Batteries
- Topographic map
- Compass
- Exchange item (optional if you don't plan on taking anything from the cache)
- Plenty of water and/or water purification tablets
- Toilet paper (just in case)
- Soap or disinfectant lotion (Many giardiasis attacks come from unwashed hands after latrine trips rather than from unpurified water.)
- Food or snacks
- Pants: high-tech outdoor fabric, wool, or polyester—no cotton
- Shirt: short-sleeved with a long-sleeved shirt as a backup, high-tech outdoor fabric, wool, or polyester—no cotton
- Fleece vest
- Bug spray
- Rain gear
- Hiking boots or tennis shoes (avoid sandals)
- Sunglasses
- Hat
- Pocketknife (This all-purpose tool's uses are too numerous to mention.)
- Waterproof matches or matches stored in a waterproof container
- Trash bags to tote out trash
- Fanny pack or day pack

Geocachers' food supplies can range from energy bars to a four-course picnic. Personal preference and the length and difficulty of the hike will determine whether you need to pack simply an energy bar or a Yogi-Bear-style spread. Whatever your nutritional needs, pick foods that do not require refrigeration; few people want to tote a cooler while hiking. Most outings can be fueled with energy bars, GORP (Good Ol' Raisins and Peanuts), peanut butter and jelly sandwiches, fruits, fruit cookies, cereal and granola bars, sardines, crackers, cheese, bagels, or pita bread. One tip, though: Avoid snacks and drinks with high sugar content. While the manic jolt of a sugar buzz may help in the short run, the inevitable sugar crash will give you a food hangover, leaving you more depleted than before you ate.

A couple more items to consider including in your knapsack are money, a first-aid kit, matches, and a smartphone. Sure, these items may seem like overkill—until you need them.

Group Geocaching

If you are geocaching with novices or children, it's a good rule of thumb to cater to the lowest common denominator, at least for the initial outing. Inexperienced outdoorspeople and kids may appreciate moderate weather, easy terrain, and an easy first find rather than an all-day slogfest that doesn't locate the cache until dusk—or not at all—and leaves everyone drenched to the bone. It's always best to ensure that their first find doesn't also share the dubious distinction of being their last.

To help others "buy into" geocaching, share the navigation duties or at least show your friends how to enter waypoints into your GPS unit and how the unit points the way, allowing them to view your screen as you approach the cache's location. Try to avoid hogging the unit and barking orders like a drill sergeant. (When sharing your GPS unit with your children, they may surprise you by knowing more about it than you do.) Working together to unravel the mystery is much more fun than following a chain of commands. When you're close to the cache, make sure to peel your eyes away from the GPS screen now and again. This may sound obvious, but don't become so focused on your GPS unit that you step off a cliff, run into a tree, or trip over a root. It's happened.

Leave No Trace

In fact, it's best to adopt Leave No Trace principles even when you're not locked in on your GPS screen. Leave nothing but footprints, and take nothing but pictures—and try to avoid leaving footprints, if possible. Most geocachers have embraced this eco-friendly approach. Knowing this fact can help you find geocaches. Let's say, for example, that you are close to a geocache. Looking one way reveals brush that would have to be bushwhacked to get through. A second choice leads through delicate ferns and wildflowers. A third option, however, is a trail leading to a rock pile. Knowing that the host would not want guests hacking and stomping their way to the geocache should help guide you down the right path.

Most hosts select a pristine site for their cache—one they hope will be as awe inspiring for the last visitor as it was for the first. Geocachers should venture into the outdoors with respect for their surroundings and leave the trail, the geocache, and its surroundings the same as or better than they found them.

Some helpful Leave No Trace principles to follow:

- **Know before you go.** Be prepared with clothing to protect you from cold, heat, or rain. Use maps to navigate so you won't get lost. Learn about the areas you visit—the more you know, the more fun you'll have.

- **Choose the right path.** Stay on the main trail and don't wander far by yourself. Do not trample or cut flowers or small trees. Once disturbed, they might not grow back.

- **Trash your trash.** Pack it in, pack it out. Put litter, including crumbs, in trash cans or carry it home. Keep water clean. Do not put soap, food, or waste in lakes or streams.

- **Leave what you find.** Leave plants, rocks, and historical items as you find them so the next person can enjoy them.

- **Respect wildlife.** Observe animals from a distance and never approach, feed, or follow them. Human food is unhealthy for all animals, and feeding them starts bad habits. Protect wildlife by storing your meals and trash. Control pets at all times or leave them at home.

- **Be kind to other visitors.** Make sure not to bother others while enjoying the outdoors. Listen to nature. Avoid making loud noises or yelling. You will see more animals if you are quiet.

Cache In, Trash Out

Many geocachers carry a small supply of trash bags. That's because they practice cache in, trash out, or CITO. The concept was born less than a year after the first cache was set out. On April 26, 2003, Groundspeak, Inc., and Magellan sponsored the First International Cache In Trash Out Day. In true Earth Day spirit, geocachers at forty-six international gatherings "picked up mountains of trash from trails and parks around the globe," according to Magellan's website.

Although the inaugural event was a huge success, one of its goals was to promote CITO as an everyday practice. As popular as geocaching is becoming, imagine how clean the outdoors could become if every geocacher picked up some trash during every outing. In terms of public relations, cleaning up and improving the areas in which geocachers play can only improve the activity's reputation. And let's face it, the act of picking up litter while you're wandering in circles talking to your GPS unit lets observers know that you're not totally insane.

7

Geo-Happenings

It should come as no surprise that geocachers like to have fun. Check through this chapter for all kinds of ways to turn your new pastime into a party.

Real-World Events

Cache In Trash Out Day (CITO): CITO is an event in which seemingly every geocaching club participates. Geocachers rally behind the idea to clean up trash when they go geocaching. CITO is simple but has a great positive impact. The idea began in fall 2000 when Groundspeak, Inc., owners of Geocaching.com, began to advocate that geocachers take along a trash bag and clean up whatever trash they see along their way. On April 26, 2003, the First International Cache In Trash Out Day was held, with clubs all over the world participating in a successful drive to remove trash from parks and other areas. Information on other ways to participate and a discussion forum dedicated to the topic are available at www .geocaching.com/cito.

Campouts: Sleeping under the stars and waking up to a full day of geocaching, hiking, and other activities makes a popular getaway for geocachers. In planning for a campout, be prepared to pay camping fees in public parks, and be aware of park rules. Campouts are a good time to hold club meetings, elections of club officials, and classes to educate club members about geocaching.

Challenges: Clubs or individuals can issue a challenge to spice things up a little bit. Challenges are exciting and competitive. When thinking up a challenge, the more creative the better. For example, timed challenges send geocachers out to find caches as fast as they can in a rush for cache treasure or points. Clubs can give out trophies or their members can earn bragging rights or receive prizes. Another example of a challenge is labeling a series of caches with codes. When an individual or team finds all of them, the achievement is recorded on a club website. Groups can CacheAcrossAmerica, which links geocaches from coast to coast in the United States. The possibilities are endless. Visit a local club website to find out more information on challenges in your area.

Educaching: This activity takes geocaching into the classroom. Actually, it works by taking students out of the classroom. The applications are endless, from solving mathematical equations to a unique approach to creative writing assignments. Using multiple caches, each hiding spot holds a key element to a math problem or story. Once all the clues are collected, the problem can be solved or the story can be written. This is also a great way to spice up field trips. When visiting a historical site, hide

Florida Cache
N 27° 49.952 • W 082° 48.767 (WGS84)
UTM: 17R E 321471 N 3079970

historical trivia that the students must find to gain a deeper appreciation to the site. (Be sure to get permission first from the property manager.) Before they know it, the students are getting exercise, learning, and having fun.

Geodating: Don't just find caches with a GPS receiver; find other people by geodating. Post a cache online with a date and time to meet, either at the cache or somewhere else for a cache hunt. Obviously, safety concerns make it necessary to have a group of single people meet up instead of just two, especially in isolated park areas.

Milestones: Once an individual or team reaches a total of one hundred, two hundred, or five hundred caches found, it's time to party! Some clubs announce these achievements on their websites or have a gathering to recognize them. Taking kids out for their first geocaching experience is also cause to celebrate: Hold a party or post pictures on a club website.

Observances: A groom can't get lost on the way to the wedding if the bride gives him a GPS unit, and neither can wedding guests. Announcing the location for a wedding, birthday party, anniversary, or other holiday online as a geocache can be a unique way to turn a celebration into an adventure.

Picnics: Everyone likes free food, and perhaps the most popular geocaching event is a picnic. Since many geocaches are placed in public parks, it makes sense to take advantage of the surroundings through a day out with fellow geocachers. A potluck picnic might be followed with other activities like face painting, door prizes, and hiking. Participants can also hunt for special caches hidden for the event. Important considerations when planning a picnic in a public park include reserving a shelter area and checking on park rules, such as whether pets are allowed. Check clubs' websites for picnic listings, or consider planning your own.

Stargazing: Know a good wide-open space with no light pollution? Post the waypoint and invite others to meet there to view a meteor shower, eclipse, or just a simple sunset. Amazing celestial events happen every year, and they're free, too! Go to www.astronomy.com for a lot more information on what's going on in the sky.

Internet Events

geo.meetup.com: Meetup is a website where people can meet and discuss any topic imaginable. Members register with the site for free, and then search for a topic of interest. Put in a zip code to find out where people in your area are meeting up to talk—in person—about a topic. The site designates a date for groups to meet every month at a certain place, such as a coffee shop. The International Geocaching Meetup Day is the second Thursday of every month. Nearly six hundred cities are currently hosting geocaching meetup days.

groups.google.com: This site allows you to start your own group or join an existing one. So, log on, peruse the group listings, and join in. Members have to register, but it's free.

groups.yahoo.com: Geocachers can join a preexisting group or create their own at Yahoo Groups. Members do have to register, but it's free.

www.livejournal.com/community/geocaching: People from all walks of life use Livejournal.com to keep their own journal online. Users can make their entries public, private, or viewable to friends only. Livejournal allows its members to create communities, including an active geocaching forum. Visitors can read and comment on entries made by fellow geocachers from all over the world or post their own experiences if they get a free account at Livejournal.com.

8
Clubs and Websites

Geocachers can find out what's going on in their own backyards by logging on to a local club's website. Exploring clubs online will reveal tips on how to deal with wildlife while geocaching, calendars of local events, and neighborly forums to discuss geocaching. Members of many of these sites have already gone to local

Geocaching is a worldwide activity. So when you're traveling, don't forget to pack your GPS unit. *Courtesy of Gail Werner*

government officials and asked permission to geocache in public parks and other places. So a quick visit to a local club's website can offer insight on rules and tips that you can use during your next outing.

The best way to transform these clubs and websites into useful tools is to visit them and participate in the activities. Leave your mark and get involved. Jump into a forum, check out some of its caches, help formulate local and national policies, or maybe set out some caches of your own. If there is no club in your area, starting a new one or creating a website is a rewarding option to keep in mind.

New clubs and sites are popping up all the time. Here's a working list of geocaching clubs and related websites throughout the world. If you find a good one you'd like to add to the list, just pencil it in.

U.S. Clubs, Groups, and Resources
Alabama
Dixie Cachers: http://x.r2designs.com/

Alaska
Alaska Geocaching: www.geocachealaska.org

Arizona
www.azgeocaching.com

Arkansas

Arkansas Geocachers Association: http://arkgeo
caching.org/

Arkansas Geocaching: www.arkansas.com/geocache

Arkansas-Missouri Geocachers Association: http://
groups.yahoo.com/group/Ark-Mo-Geocachers/

Ozark Mountains: groups.yahoo.com/group/ozmtn
geocachers

The Associated Arkansas Geocachers (TAAG):
www.arkgeocachers.org

California

Geocaching in Thousand Oaks: www.denniscoins.com
/geocaching

Geocachers of the Bay Area: www.thegba.net/

High Desert Geocachers: http://highdesertgeocachers
.com/

Northstate Unusual Treasure Seekers (NUTS): http://
groups.yahoo.com/group/nuts/

River City Geocaching and Dining Society: www.rcgds
.net/Socal 4x4 Geocachers: www.socal4x4geocachers
.org/

Poison Oak Cachers (Central Coast): http://poisonoak
cachers.com/

California Geocaching: http://groups.yahoo.com/
group/california_geocaching/

Central Coast Geocachers of California: http://groups
.yahoo.com/group/ccgca/

Colorado
Geocaching Colorado: www.geocachingcolo.com/
Colorado State Forests: http://parks.state.co.us/Parks
StateForest/Geocaching/

Connecticut
Connecticut Caching Community: http://ctcachers
.com/
Southern New England Geocachers: www.sne
geocachers.com/

Delaware
Delaware Geocachers: www.geocachingde.net/c/
Delaware State Parks: www.destateparks.com
/activities/geocaching/index.asp

Florida
Florida Geocaching: http://floridageocaching.com/
Florida Geocaching Association: www.tagfla.com/
Space Coast Geocachers: www.spacecoastgeocachers
.com/
Geocaching Club of the Villages: www.geocachingthe
villages.com/
Northeast Florida Geocaching Association: www.nef
ga.com/
Tallahassee Area Geocachers (TAG): www.tagfla.com/

Georgia

Georgia Geocachers Association: www.ggaonline.org
Georgia Hikes: www.georgiahikes.com/geocache/
Chattahoochee Valley Cachers: http://groups.yahoo
.com/group/CVCachers/

Hawaii

Hawaii Geocachers and GPS Enthusiasts: www.light
fantastic.org/gps
True Aloha: http://truealoha.com/blog/category/
geocaching-in-hawaii/

Idaho

Idaho Geocachers: www.idahogeocachers.org

Illinois

Geocachers of Northeastern Illinois (GONIL):
www.gonil.org
Central Illinois Geocaching Association (CIGA):
www.cigacache.org/index.php

Iowa

Iowa Geocachers Organization:
www.iowageocachers.org

Kansas

Kansas Geocaching: www.kansasgeocaching.com

Kentucky

Geocachers of Kentucky: www.geocky.org

River Valley Geocachers: http://rvgc.net/index.php

Louisiana

North Louisiana Geocachers: www.nelageo.net

Michigan Cache
N 45° 02.613 • W 083° 26.950
(WGS84)
UTM: 17T E 307114 N 4990706

Maryland

Maryland Geocaching Society: www.mdgps.org

Massachusetts

Southern New England Geocachers: www.snegeocachers.com

Michigan

Michigan Geocaching Organization: www.mi-geocaching.org

Northern Michigan Geocachers: www.nmg-geocaching.org

Minnesota

Minnesota Geocaching Association: www.mngca.org

Mississippi
Mississippi Geocachers Association: www.msga.net

Missouri
St. Louis Area Geocachers Association: www.slaga.org
River Valley Geocachers: http://rvgc.net/index.php
Arkansas-Missouri Geocachers: http://groups.yahoo
.com/group/Ark-Mo-Geocachers/

Montana
Big Sky Cachers: www.bigskycachers.com

Nebraska
Wyoming-Nebraska Area Geocachers: www.wnag.net
Nebraskache: http://groups.yahoo.com/group/
nebraskache/

Nevada
Nevada Geocaching Association: www.nevada
geocaching.com
Great Basin and Sierra Geocachers: www.gbesgeo.org

New Hampshire
Granite State Geocachers Community: www.granite
stategeocachers.org/community/index.php
Southern New England Geocachers: www.sne
geocachers.com

New Mexico
Cache New Mexico: http://nmgeocaching.com/wp/
Geocaching New Mexico: groups.yahoo.com/group
/NM_Geo

New York
New York Geocaching Organization: www.ny-geo
caching.org
Long Island Geocaching Organization: www.ligeo
caching.com
New York Capital Area Geocachers: www.geo
cachingny.org
Southern Tier Geocachers: http://groups.yahoo.com/
group/Southerntiergeocachers/

North Carolina
Triangle Geocachers: groups.yahoo.com/group/
TriangleGeocachers

North Dakota
Wolf Draw Geocache: http://eduscapes.com/geo
caching/wolf.htm

Ohio
Geocaching in Ohio: www.gcinohio.org
Ohio, Kentucky, and Indiana Cachers: www.okic.org
Miami Valley Geocachers: www.mvgeo.com
Gem City Geocachers: www.gemcitygeo.org

Northwest Ohio Geocachers: www.nwogeo.org

Oklahoma
Oklahoma Geocaching: http://okgeocaching.net/

Oregon
Oregon Geocaching: www.oregongeocaching.com
Portland Geocaching: www.pdxgeocaching.com
Emerald Valley Cachers: www.gotcache.com
Southern Oregon Geocaching: www.sogeo.org

Pennsylvania
Southeastern Pennsylvania Geocachers: www.sepa
g.mocadeki.com/postnuke
Pittsburgh Area Geocaching Association: www.wpa
ga.com
Harrisburg Area Cachers: http://groups.yahoo.com/
group/Harrisburg_Geocachers/
Northwestern Pennsylvania Geocachers: groups.yahoo
.com/group/NWPAGeoCachers
**Three Rivers Informal Geocaching Organization
(TRIGO):** http://groups.yahoo.com/group/tri-go/

Rhode Island
Southern New England Geocachers: www.snegeo
cachers.com

South Carolina
South Carolina Geocachers Association: www.isc
ga.org/a/

South Dakota
South Dakota Game, Fish and Parks: http://gfp.sd.gov
/to-do/geocaching/default.aspx

Tennessee
Geocachers of Southeast Tennessee: www.geoset.org
Middle Tennessee Geocachers Club: www.mtgc.org
Geocachers of West Tennessee: www.gowt.org/news
/index.php
River Valley Geocachers: http://rvgc.net/index.php
Greater East Tennessee Geocaching Club: www.get
gc.org

Texas
Texas Geocaching: www.txga.net
Houston Geocaching Society: http://hgcs.org/
Central Texas Geocachers: http://groups.yahoo.com
/group/CentralTexasGeocachers/
Heart of Texas Geocaching: http://hotgeocaching
.homestead.com/
Greater Abilene Geocachers: www.greaterabilene
ga.com

Utah
Utah Association of Geocachers: www.utah
geocachers.com

Vermont
Southern New England Geocachers:
www.snegeocachers.com

Virginia
Central Virginia Geocaching Association:
http://groups.yahoo.com/group/centralva
geocaching/
Fredericksburg Geocachers: http://groups.yahoo
.com/group/FredericksburgGeocachers/
Hampton Roads Geocaching: http://groups.yahoo
.com/group/Geocaching-HamptonRoadsVA/
Northern Virginia Geocaching Organization:
www.novago.org/wp/

Washington
Washington State Geocaching Association: www.ws
gaonline.org/forums/index.php

Wisconsin
Wisconsin Geocaching Club: www.wi-geocaching.com

West Virginia
West Virginia State Parks: www.wvstateparks.com
/recreation/geocache.htm

Wyoming
Wyoming and Nebraska Area Geocachers (WNAG):
www.wnag.net

International Clubs
Australia: geocaching.com.au
Belgium: www.geocache.be/web/nl/index.htm
Canada (British Columbia): www.bcgeocaching.com/
Canada (Atlantic coast): www.atlanticgeocaching.com/
Canada (Manitoba): www.mbgeocaching.ca/index.html
Canada (Quebec): www.geocaching-qc.com/index
.php/accueil
Czechoslovakia: www.geocaching.cz/news.php
Denmark: www.geocaching.dk
Estonia: www.geopeitus.ee
Finland: www.geocache.fi/
France: www.geocaching-france.com/
Germany: www.geocaching.de/
Great Britain: www.gagb.co.uk/gagb/
Hungary: www.geocaching.hu
Ireland: www.geocachingireland.com/
Italy: www.geocaching-italia.com/
Japan (Okinawa): www.okicache.com/
Lithuania: www.gps.lt/geocaching/%20
Netherlands: www.geocaching.nl/index/
New Zealand: www.gps.org.nz/
Poland: www.geocaching.angielski.co.uk/

Portugal: http://geocaching-pt.net/
Romania: www.rejtekhely.ro/
Russia: www.geocaching.ru
Slovak Republic: www.geocaching.sk/
Switzerland/Lichtenstein: www.swissgeocache.ch/
Tasmania: tas.geocaching.com.au

Can you geocache in Paris? Oui! *Courtesy of Gail Werner*

General Websites

www.geocaching.com: This is the central clearinghouse for geocaching. Millions of geocachers go to the site to access more than one million geocaches worldwide, get the latest news, post event notices, and see the latest advances.

www.navicache.com: Navicache lists caches, clubs, maps, and GPS manufacturers—a veritable wealth of geocaching information.

www.brillig.com/geocaching/maps.shtml: Buxley's Waypoint lists geocaches around the world. The site includes statistics on the number of geocachers and maps of cache locations.

www.eduscapes.com/geocaching/kids.htm: This site gives advice and ideas to teachers and parents on how to make geocaching a great learning experience for kids.

www.nps.gov: The National Park Service website has seemingly endless information on U.S. national parks and their policies.

babelfish.altavista.com: Although not related to geocaching, the search engine offers a very valuable service for Internet users. Users can translate a block of text by copying it and pasting it, or have an entire website translated just by entering the web address. It's quite handy, especially if you want to find caches abroad or just want to find information on the Internet.

www.geology.enr.state.nc.us/gis/latlon.html: Use this site to convert decimal degrees to degrees, minutes, and seconds, or vice versa.

www.maptools.com: An introduction to latitude and longitude coordinates, tools for mapping coordinates with a GPS, and other tutorials are available here.

http://earth.google.com: Simply put, Google Earth allows you to view every spot on Earth. Heck, it even allows you to explore the moon and Mars.

www.bingmaps.com/maps: Bing maps allows users to plan routes through view streets maps, aerial and bird's-eye view, and 3-D cities.

www.mapquest.com: Mapquest is a free Internet version of Rand McNally, offering driving cues for the directionally challenged. The site can map one area, or map the route between two points, and includes an easy-to-use road trip planner.

GPS Units and Software

Garmin: www.garmin.com. Garmin products are geared to the outdoors, and its website is mindful of geocaching. The site allows visitors to easily compare Garmin products to competitors' units. For specifics on geocaching go to www.garmin.com/outdoor/geocaching.

Magellan: www.magellangps.com. Magellan is a regular supporter of geocaching-themed events and websites. Part of its website is dedicated to geocaching and helps visitors match the best products to their needs.

DeLorme: www.delorme.com. The mapping leader makes some quality handheld GPS units. And not surprisingly, the units come equipped with some really great maps.

Topografix: www.topografix.com. Here you will find EasyGPS and ExpertGPS, two programs that allow you to work with waypoints easily. After creating or editing a waypoint, users can transfer it to selected GPS systems. There are many possible ways to use this software, including geocaching. Other programs on the Topografix site include GeoBuddy, which allows you to convert files to different formats, and PanTerra, which helps you manage your waypoints more efficiently. The site has many resources and help files in case of any problems. Although EasyGPS is available for free, other Topografix programs are only available for a free thirty-day trial.

FUGAWI: www.fugawi.com. This is the place to find programs that are packed with useful features—allowing you, for instance, to create digital maps that reflect your position as you move. The software must be purchased, but a smaller trial version can be downloaded.

Safety

www.findmespot.com: These satellite messengers can transmit satellite photos, indicating your location to folks who are following your trek. Another push of a button can alert emergency services that you need help.

Mapping Resources

Google Earth: http://earth.google.com/outreach/tutorial_ importgps.html. The site can connect you to one of the most amazing mapping resources ever created. The page even comes with an easy-to-follow tutorial to get you started.

Google Earth Blog: www.gearthblog.com. This blog keeps folks current on the latest news on Google Earth.

Map My Ride and Map My Hike: www.mapmyride.com and www.mapmyhike.com. These sites allow geocachers, cycling, and hiking enthusiasts to literally map, archive, and share their rides and hikes. They calculate mileage, elevation, and more.

EveryTrail.com: www.everytrail.com. This site allows you to map a trip with your phone or GPS, add trip photos to your map as you go, add maps to your blog, and more.

The National Geodetic Survey: www.ngs.noaa.gov. This site provides survey information for each county in the United States, a searchable database of benchmarks, and an interactive mapping web page.

Trails.com: www.trails.com. This site is a great guide to many outdoor activities from finding trails to making travel plans and selecting gear. It also hosts Topozone, a provider of topographic maps of the United States in seven different scales. Users must sign up for a free trial or purchase a subscription to request, personalize, or download a map. For free, the site lets you easily look up landmarks such as bridges, towers, or cemeteries in any state and gives the coordinates for the sites.

Maptech: www.maptech.com. Maptech is a supplier of land, aeronautical, marine maps, aerial photos, software, and more.

DeLorme: www.delorme.com. This Maine-based company provides flexible mapping software products that cover all fifty states in one package for consumers and professionals.

9
Cachionary 2.0

No activity would be complete without its own lexicon—and geocaching is no exception. Like most dictionaries, this cachionary contains only the terms currently in general use. So let's call it Cachionary 2.0 (since this is the second edition of this book). Dedicated geocachers will, no doubt, continue to pencil in many additional terms as the activity grows.

At the rate geocaching is catching on, terms in this ever-expanding cachionary will eventually find their way into everyday language and be found in mainstream dictionaries such as those compiled by Webster's and Oxford.

Since geocaching is a blend of many navigational activities, some historical terms have been included. After all, the batteries in your GPS unit may someday run out, and it will be helpful to have a working knowledge of some good ol' map and compass terms.

Welcome to Geo-Speak
1/1: Shorthand indicating cache difficulty/terrain rating.

ATCF: A logbook term meaning "as the crow flies"; mileage based solely on point-to-point, not including ravines, rivers, roads, etc.

Adoption: In terms of geocaching, taking over abandoned geocaches and tending them as your own or finding appropriate hosts for them. Adoption can happen only after all attempts to contact the original hosts have failed.

Agonic line: The place where declination is zero. The agonic line runs from the Great Lakes to Florida.

Aiming off: Pointing a compass to the left and right of the destination to create a planned error factor.

Almanac data: Satellite constellation information transmitted by each satellite. GPS receivers must acquire this information before they can begin to calculate a position.

Antenna: GPS receivers have either an internal or an external antenna. To help boost receiver reception, many receivers have external antenna adaptors.

Archiving: Deleting a cache from website listings. Geocache owners can archive sites if they are not going to maintain them any longer. Website managers archive caches if the caches have been abandoned, if they feel the cache does not meet prescribed guidelines, or if it has been placed illegally, such as at a national park.

Attack point: A landmark on a map that is easy to identify while in the field, such as a plateau, river, or road.

Back bearing: Also known as a "reciprocal bearing," this is the direction opposite (180 degrees) from where you arrived.

Batteries: Manna for GPS units. They gobble batteries like Yogi Bear eats picnic baskets, draining their life in four to twenty-four hours. Always carry spares.

Bearing: The angle measured in degrees between a line heading north from your position and a line heading toward a landmark.

Benchmarks: Geodetic control points permanently affixed around the United States to facilitate land surveying, civil engineering, and mapping. Vertical control points can be small brass or aluminum disks, or concrete posts. Horizontal control points can be disks or posts as well as radio towers, water towers, church spires, or mountaintops.

BYOP: A logbook term meaning "bring your own pen."

Bee dance: Also known as the drunken bee dance; the final quivers of geocachers as they close in on a cache.

Cache (pronounced cash): In terms of geocaching, it's a hidden container filled with a logbook, writing utensil, and sometimes prizes. Generically speaking, caches are any hidden stores of food and/or equipment.

Cache cams (or web cam caches): Web cams that serve double duty as geocaches. The treasures at these sites are pictures of you standing in front of the web cam.

Cachuration: An undesirable situation in which too many caches are located close together, saturating the area.

Cairn: A heap of stones used as a landmark. These piles should be knocked down after their use to remove all traces of your journey.

Cardinal points: North, south, east, and west.

Century club: Geocachers who have located a hundred caches.

CITO: Cache in, trash out. A common practice of geocachers who clean up as they cache. Anytime you travel into the wild, you should leave it a better place than you found it.

Compass: A necessary backup for your GPS unit—and luckily, one that does not require batteries.

Constellation: An arrangement of objects such as stars. In terms of GPS, it refers to an arrangement of satellites.

Contour lines: Lines that mark differences in elevation on topographic maps.

Coordinated Universal Time (UTC): A composite time scale used by GPS satellites based on input from atomic clocks and a time scale referenced to the earth's rate of rotation.

Coordinates: A set of numbers, such as the intersection of latitude and longitude, that accurately specifies location.

Datum: Something used as the basis for calculating and measuring. For geocachers, datums are different calculations for determining longitude and latitude for a given location. Currently, geocaching uses the WGS84 datum for all caches. (Caution: Many maps still use NAD27 datum. Always check the datum before entering coordinates into your GPS.)

Dead reckoning: In sailing or aeronautics, it's the determination of position without the aid of celestial observation. Also known as guesswork, it's used when you forget to bring a compass and your GPS receiver runs out of batteries.

Declination: The difference between true north and magnetic north. This varies from 20 degrees west in Maine to 21 degrees east in Washington. In Alaska the difference can be as much as 30 degrees.

Digitalfish: A signature item that has a unique identifier that allows it to be tracked online.

Dilution of precision (DOP): A measurement of the quality of satellite geometry. Poor satellite geometry means that the satellites are bunched together or in a straight line and cannot provide an accurate reading. Typically, the larger the DOP, the poorer the geometry.

Divine cache: Caches placed at degree confluences.

DNF: A logbook term meaning "did not find."

Doghouse: Slang for the printed arrow inside the housing of an orienteering compass. Also, the place you'll find yourself when you spend too much time geocaching without your spouse.

Educaching: Using geocaching to enhance a learning environment. Examples of educaching include students finding multiple caches to learn more about a historic site during a field trip, gathering elements of a math problem to solve it, or collecting components of a story that, when collected, will tell a colorful tale.

Estimated time of arrival (ETA): The time you will arrive at your destination, based on your speed of travel and distance to be covered. See doghouse to get an idea of what happens when you give someone the wrong ETA.

FTF: A logbook acronym meaning "first to find."

The Force: The sixth-sense of being able to spot locations likely to conceal a cache.

Geocoding: Putting your location into coordinates.

Geocoins: Custom-minted and numbered coins that are designed to provide geocachers with a prize that is collectible, tradable, and trackable. One manufacturer calls them the "ultimate cache prize."

Geomuggle: A non-geocacher. Adapted from the term for nonmagical people used in the Harry Potter books.

Pennsylvania Cache
N 40° 10.132 • W 075° 42.383
(WGS84)
UTM: 18T E 439852 N 4446739

GLONASS: Global Navigation Satellite System, the navigation system developed by the former Soviet Union that is similar to GPS.

GPS: Global Positioning System. The system of twenty-four satellites orbiting 12,000 miles above the earth that work with GPS receivers to locate the coveted caches. At any given time there are five of these satellites above the horizon ready to help you find your way.

GPSr: Slang for a GPS receiver. Equipment to receive GPS signals for use in navigation.

The Great American GPS Stash Hunt (or GPS Stash Hunt): The original name for geocaching. Early players thought the name sounded too seedy and changed it.

Grid: A coordinate system used for position measurements that projects the earth on a flat surface using square zones created by sets of parallel lines.

Ground zero: Also known as gz; the exact point where the coordinates of your GPS unit match the coordinates of the cache in which you are seeking.

Handrails: Recognizable geographic features such as canyons, lakeshores, rivers, or roads that serve as guides allowing you to travel without referencing your GPS unit or map.

Hitchhiker: Items placed in a cache that have been designated to travel to other caches. Sometimes they are accompanied with logbooks to track their travels.

Initialization: The process that a GPS receiver uses to collect its bearings, if you will, when it hasn't been used in a while, when it has been moved hundreds of miles since it was last turned on, or when it has lost its UTC (see Coordinated Universal Time).

Intercardinal points: Northeast, northwest, southeast, and southwest.

Landmark: A physical location identified by a feature such as a mountain peak or a trail intersection. Some GPS receivers substitute landmark for the term waypoint, which is a location described with coordinates and used for GPS navigation.

Latitude: The angular distance north or south from the earth's equator measured through 90 degrees.

Longitude: The angular distance measured on a great circle of reference from the intersection of the adopted zero meridian with this reference circle to the similar intersection of the meridian passing through the object.

Logging another find.

LPC: A logbook term meaning "lamp post cache." A common hiding place for microcaches.

Lubber line: The line or reference mark on a compass where bearings are read.

MKH: A logbook term meaning "magnetic key holder"; commonly used as a microcache.

Map datum: Simply put, this term refers to how the spatial foundation of a map relates to the actual area it represents. NAD27 is the most common datum for North

American maps. WGS84 is the mapping standard for GPS. Some countries use other datums. In fact, there are more than a hundred datums worldwide. Make sure the map datum you use matches that used by your receiver.

Memory: The more memory your GPS has, the more waypoints and route information it can store. An average unit can store up to twenty waypoints and five routes. Receivers should have a backup system that allows you to change batteries so you don't lose your waypoints and custom settings—especially while you're looking for a cache.

Microcache: Small geocaches typically used for caches hidden in urban settings. Examples include Altoids tins affixed to metal surfaces with magnets, small tubes stashed in hedges, or microcache stones hidden in rock piles.

Multipath interference: Satellite signals bouncing off objects before reaching your GPS unit. Wet leaves or areas of tall buildings, sometimes called urban canyons, can interfere with the signal. The receiver's antenna must have a clear view of the sky to operate efficiently.

NAD27: North American Datum 1927. This is the most common datum in North America. It's used on U.S. Geological Survey (USGS) maps and U.S. Department of Agriculture (USDA) Forest Service maps. Since many maps still use this datum, always check the datum before entering the coordinates into your GPS receiver.

When you get close, it's time to turn up your sleuthing skills.

Nano: A cache smaller than a microcache. Some are as small as a pencil eraser.

NIAH: A logbook term meaning "needle in a haystack." A tiny cache hidden in a location with many potential hiding places.

North: There are actually three norths: true, or geographic; magnetic, or the direction the compass needle points; and grid, or the direction the grid lines run on a topographic map.

Orienteering: A competitive sport, nicknamed "running with cunning," that combines running or hiking with locating control points with a compass.

P&G: A logbook term meaning "park and grab." An easy-access, easy-to-find cache for which you can park your car nearby.

Power trail: Also known as a cache machine; a path with numerous, easy caches hidden every 1/10th of a mile.

Pregridding: Connecting the UTM or the latitude/longitude tick marks found on the margin of a topographic map before venturing into the wilderness. This helps identify waypoints and allows you to store them into your GPS unit before leaving home.

Receiver channels: The number of channels from which a GPS unit can receive information. The more satellite signals your GPS unit is receiving, the better its accuracy. It needs to pick up a minimum of three to determine position, and four to determine location and altitude.

Route: The path between two waypoints.

Scale: The relationship between a map and actual ground distance.

Selective Availability (SA): An error deliberately placed into GPS signals by the Defense Department intended to deny military adversaries—and, consequently, recreational GPS users—access to precise position information. The signal was turned off May 1, 2000.

Signature item: An item found inside a cache that is identified with a specific geocacher or group of geocachers.

SL: A logbook term meaning "signed log."

Spoiler: Information giving away details of a cache and potentially spoiling the find for others.

Symbols: Icons on maps that primarily depict human-made features.

TFTC: A logbook term meaning "thanks for the cache."

TFTH: A logbook term meaning "thanks for the hunt."

TNLN: A logbook acronym meaning "took nothing, left nothing." It's usually used in logbooks by those who enjoy the thrill of hunting more than claiming a prize.

TNLNSL: A logbook term meaning "took nothing, left nothing, signed logbook."

Topographic map (topo): A map that shows an area's "ridges, ravines, and all things between" in three dimensions with the aid of contour lines.

Track logging: A feature on GPS receivers that allows you to record your route as you travel.

Travel bug: A hitchhiker whose travels or progress can be monitored on Geocaching.com. Those who plant travel

Travel bugs are items that travel from cache to cache (note the bug on the attached card). Their movement can be tracked on the web.

bugs can give their bugs any goal they desire. The creativity of the task—say, "Travel to twelve states in one year"—is limited only by the imaginations of those who place them. Also see hitchhiker.

Travel bug hotel: A cache that serves as an exchange point for travel bugs.

Travel bug prison: A travel bug hotel that requires replacing as many travel bugs as you take. They are called prisons or jails because travel bugs can sometimes get stuck there.

Triangulation: Taking three measurements to pinpoint location. In terms of GPS, using three satellite signals to locate you and your GPS unit. Using more than three satellites increases the accuracy of the reading.

Universal Transverse Mercator (UTM): A coordinate system—an alternative to latitude and longitude—that uses distances from standard reference points to grid maps into 1,000-meter (1-kilometer) intervals. So rather than listing coordinates by hours, minutes, and seconds, UTM coordinates are expressed by meters. Visualizing distance in terms of a meter stick is easier than by minutes and seconds. UTM references can be found in the margins of USGS maps.

UPS or UPR: A logbook term meaning "unnatural pile of sticks/unnatural pile of rocks"; a telltale sign of a hidden cache.

Virtual cache: A virtual cache is a trek to the location itself. Virtual caches may not have a bucket with prizes, but they do offer beautiful or unspoiled views.

Warning system: This feature allows your GPS unit to cry out for help, indicating poor satellite reception or problems with the unit itself. Some units beep while others display an icon.

Watch list: A list of users who are watching a specific hitchhiker or cache.

Wayfarer: Individuals who wish to participate in an orienteering meet in a noncompetitive manner. Also called a map-walker.

Waypoint: A location described with coordinates and used for GPS navigation. Some GPS units substitute the term landmark for waypoint. Receivers identify these points with short names using descriptions of five or six letters and/or numbers.

Wide Area Augmentation System (WAAS): In a nutshell, WAAS increases accuracy and signal availability. This system sends differential correction and integrity messages via geostationary earth-orbiting satellites at the same frequencies as GPS.

World Geodetic System of 1984 (WGS84): The GPS mapping standard. Some countries use different datums. Always check before geocaching in other countries.

YACIDKA: A logbook term meaning "yet another cemetery I didn't know about."

YAPIDNA: A logbook term meaning "yet another park I didn't know about."

INDEX

Great Britain, 99
Greater Abilene Geocachers, 97
Greater East Tennessee
    Geocaching Club, 97
Groundspeak, Inc., 9, 81, 83

H
Hampton Roads Geocaching, 98
Harrisburg Area Cachers, 96
Hawaii Geocachers and GPS
    Enthusiasts, 92
Heart of Texas Geocaching, 97
Hide-and-Seek game, 60
High Desert Geocachers, 90
Houston Geocaching Society, 97
Hungary, 99

I
Idaho Geocachers, 92
Illinois, 92
Internationaler
    Volkssportverband, 70
Iowa Geocachers
    Organization, 92
Ireland, 99
Irish, Jeremy, 9
Italy, 99

J
James, Dan, 49
Japan (Okinawa), 99
Jeep 4x4 Geocaching
    Challenge, 60

Just 4 Openers game, 60–61

K
Kansas Geocaching, 92
Kennedy, President John F., 1
Kentucky, 93

L
latitude and longitude
    coordinates. *See* waypoints
Leave No Trace principles,
    79–82
letterbox hybrid, 62
letterboxing, 61–62
Letterboxing in America, 61, 62
Lithuania, 99
Livejournal, 87
Long Island Geocaching
    Organization, 95
Louisiana, 93
Lowrance, 9, 31

M
Magellan, 9, 30, 31, 81, 103
maps
    Bing maps, 102
    datum, 32
    DeLorme, 9, 30, 31, 103, 105
    Mapmyhike.com, 104
    Mapmyride.com, 104
    mapping skills, 16, 35
    Mapquest, 102
    Maptech, 105

ABOUT THE AUTHOR

Layne Cameron is an avid outdoorsman who has authored or coauthored five books and more than three hundred articles for national magazines and newspapers, including *Scouting* magazine and *Boys' Life.* The Hoosier native has enjoyed assignments ranging from riding and mapping Indiana's mountain bike trails to ballooning New Mexico's redrock canyons, from ice fishing Minnesota's walleye-laden lakes to barefoot waterskiing in Florida's tea-colored waterways.

Cameron's first exposure to geocaching was a January 2001 brief in *Outside* magazine ("If You Hide It, They Will Come"). Later, while mountain biking in southern Indiana, Cameron spotted a GPS-toting hiker who at first glance seemed to have lugged along a five-gallon bucket. After further inquiry, Cameron confirmed that he had spotted his first geocacher, who had performed the exchange ritual and claimed a small prize as his own.

Cameron works as the science and technology writer for Michigan State University.